Character Breakdown

Zawe Ashton

Chatto & Windus
LONDON

1 3 5 7 9 10 8 6 4 2

Chatto & Windus, an imprint of Vintage,
20 Vauxhall Bridge Road,
London SW1V 2SA

Chatto & Windus is part of the Penguin Random House group of companies
whose addresses can be found at global.penguinrandomhouse.com

Penguin
Random House
UK

First published in the United Kingdom by Chatto & Windus in 2019

www.penguin.co.uk

A CIP catalogue record for this book is available from the British Library

ISBN 9781784740795

All images © Zawe Ashton, excluding p.218 © WENN Rights Ltd /
Alamy Stock Photo.

Typeset in 11 / 16 pt Palatino
by Integra Software Services Pvt. Ltd, Pondicherry

Printed and bound in Great Britain by Clays Ltd, Elcograf S.p.A.

Penguin Random House is committed to a sustainable future for
our business, our readers and our planet. This book is made
from Forest Stewardship Council® certified paper.

For
Auntie S and Auntie R

Roll up, roll up! The circus is in town! See the elephants fly, trapeze artists conquer death-defying feats and – of course – the den of freaks. The real star of our show, ladies and gentlemen – and back by the most popular demand – Lana the Lady of Many Adjectives! Yes, look amazed, for she is what makes our circus truly great! Known as 'The Human Chameleon' in some of our native constituencies, 'La Dame de beaucoup de couleurs' in Paris of course, 'Oku no keiyoshi no josei' in Hong Kong, and 'mwanamke vivumishiwengi' to our friends in the Swahili-speaking nations of the African continent. She's a sight to behold, and for those of you returning, well, how she will amaze even on a second, third, fourth viewing! Behold how she shapeshifts from one recognisable form to another, ladies and gentlemen! So seamlessly does she transform, many have questioned whether it is white magic. But like her colleague and good friend, and second-most popular act in the den of freaks, my good people, Bonnie the Bearded Lady – yes, another cheer for our bearded princess! What a gal! What a gal – much like Bonnie, this is something our precious chameleon was born to, a gift from the high and powerful! We have it here on these humble shores to wow you with today.

I joined this circus as a boy, ladies and gentlemen. I've seen all there is to see. There's not a freak I haven't witnessed up close. Mottle and Modrigal, the conjoined twins with a passion for yodelling, left on our doorstep in a wicker basket with a note that read 'Do as God would bid.' We gave those girl-children a second chance at life under this big top. Yes, roll right up, get nice and warm now, ladies and gentlemen, huddle

1

together, as I tell you the story of Ariel – the mermaid rescued from the wreckage of a washed-up trawler. We found her gasping for air among the bodies of good men and brought her here. It was the happiest of coincidences that we had the human-sized tank for Klaus the Krusader's pirate escape trick in the back of our wagon! I'll never forget the gasp she gave when she plunged into that water, ladies and gents. Never trust a mermaid! people warned. She's a special part of our family and was our most unique freak act ... Until now. I wouldn't be lying when I said that Lady Lana of many colours, many names, many skins, is the most special, most unique of all the lady freaks we've had here. Ever. None have moved me, ladies and gentlemen, like the spectacle of Lana. That's it, huddle together, Cammy the Contortionist will put your pounds in the glass jar. You'll see her do something else entirely with that very jar in just a little while's time. Whoa-ho! That very jar!

The illumination, folks, that Lana has provided us with since she joined our merry band, is like nothing I've experienced in the circus before. There's no one performance the same. And how our paths came to cross is no less exceptional than any of my other girl freaks. Driving through the desert one night, a sandstorm kicked up, so thick I stopped the wagon. No show is so important as the safety of my flock. I threw my voice back as far as it would go, hoping the message to bed down for the night would travel. I hurled my voice into the wind until it was hoarse and still no reply. A grave worry came over me. I gave one more call that took so much strength, ladies and gents, I nearly passed out and loosed my mare from her harness! Suddenly, through the whistling of the wind, I heard a voice – it carried on the moving sand. But when it reached my ear, I discovered to my horror – it was my echo. My own voice thrown back at my wagon! Well, this was most curious as the land was flat. There were no mountains, valleys or even anthills for my voice to bounce off. My fear was that Echo, that ungodly sprite, might have hitched herself to our wagon – causing all types of her usual chaos! My troupe are fragile folks.

I jumped from my wagon, tying the filly to a cactus, my scarf about my eyes in case the sand blasted them from their sockets. It was a night sent from Lucifer's hand to test us. I went in search of the other wagons. As I walked, hands to the wind, I began to make out a figure approaching. 'Echo, you little nymph, release us from this havoc!' There was no answer. Slowly, it seemed to me that this figure wasn't that of a sprite, but that of a man. Straining my eyes even more, trying to identify the oncoming figure, I cried out again. 'Echo?' My voice bounced back. 'Damn you, Echo! You know there ain't any room for you in this here troupe! Your mischief has no place here. Now let us alone so we can sleep off this storm!' No sooner had the words left my mouth, the figure that had been silhouetted in the dust was as close as the tip of the nose on my face. Nothing could have prepared me for what happened next, the most extraordinary encounter I can commit to record, ladies and gentlemen. Just as I had been communicating with a voice that was a dead ringer for my own, I was now face-to-face with my own image. The face, hands, hair, body, clothes were – mine. A true reflection.

Convinced the lack of food and water had finally done me in,
I took the doppelgänger to be a powerful mirage and resolved
to find the rest of the wagons. At that moment, our very own
Bonnie the Bearded Lady appeared through the sand. She
called out to me and no sooner had she opened her mouth
than it rang out in an echo exactly as before. No sooner had
the echo resounded, the vision I had dismissed shapeshifted
into a true likeness of Bonnie in front of our eyes. Her face,
her body, her beard, her torn dress, her voice – reflected
exactement! Ladies and gentleman, as someone party to
my grand share of illusions over time, this was the most
accomplished act of any I had ever seen. Bonnie cried out,
her nerves shot as mine had been moments before. More of
our troupe emerged through the fog, responding to Bonnie's
blood-curdling cry. And as quickly as each one came, was as
quickly as the creature changed. Klaus the Krusader – the
creature took on his exact form, Polly the parrot to boot!
Strong Man fell to his knees when the creature took on his
curly moustache, the tattoo of his mother over his heart. The
screams and hollers of disbelief kept every circus girl and
boy coming to the place and there wasn't a clown, sideshow
act or animal that it couldn't emulate. As those who had
fainted were brought about with smelling potions, the sand
still swirling through us, I took my moment, grabbing the
creature by the shoulders.

'Who. Are. You?!'

Lo and behold, the creature looked me dead in the eyes
and dropped its final simulation as quickly and easily as the
curtain might fall at the end of a play. Another round of

gasps went up when we saw what lay beneath these energetic transformations. A young woman, barely out of girlhood. A simple shift hanging loosely from her fragile collarbones. Her hair, arms, legs, eyes all registered as human. A human woman.

'My name is Lana. I am whoever you want me to be.'

Her voice was soft and yet could cut through a sandstorm.

Why was this eighth wonder stranded alone in the desert? She was destined to come with us.

The reception we received the following night with the grand unveiling of our precious Lana, the Lady of a million Adjectives, went down in freak-show history. She held a mirror up to humanity so clear, there was not a man or woman unsusceptible to her power. We ate well that night, ladies and gentlemen, and many of us tried our first drops of champagne.

Ladies and gentlemen, you've indulged me. We are now sold out! What a beautiful crowd you are. It's warming up, it's warming up now. I know you won't be let down by our main attraction here tonight, we've been all over the world and never failed to shock, awe and of course move. For your amazement and pleasure, she's the Human Chameleon, our precious Changeling, she is – the Lady of Many Adjectives!!!

Another fanfare please!

Keep that applause coming, ladies and gentlemen, she's the most timid of sideshow starlets, the most humble of wonders! Lana! The Lady of Many Adjectives! Keep those hands clapping, don't stop the clapping! Another fanfare, please!

A frail woman enters from the side of the arena, her ribs concertina under the delicate fabric of her slip.

Transform for us, you sensitive beauty! Famed freak! Pearl of our world-famous production! This woman is anything you want her to be! You won't be disappointed! Lana! Lana!

Her ashen feet drag, leaving tracks in the sawdust.

Character: Cute Little Girl, 6 yrs.
Breakdown: Cute little girl, 6 yrs.
Project: Long-running children's TV series.
Notes from casting: Please only submit girls who can take direction.

The camera rolls.

This is a world populated by men and lights.

So much light around me it feels like I'm on my own.

Apart from the camera.

It's a little black eye.

It follows me wherever I go.

I've got new clothes and someone has done my hair.

'Do you want some make-up?'

'Like my dolls?'

'Yeah!'

When people talk *to* me, they use *my* name. When they talk *about* me they use another name. The name of the character.

When they say 'cut', it means stop, and when they say 'action', it means go.

'Action' means be the character, someone else.

'Cut' means be myself.

'So cute!'

I have to kneel down, wind a watch and smile. That's my part.

'Cut!'

It's so hot.

Someone gives me a Coca-Cola in the bottle.

'Is this for me?'

Do I drink it?

I hold on to it for a long time. I can hear people start to laugh on the other side of the lights.

I'm so thirsty.

Is this for me or for her?

'You're so cute!'

I don't remember Coca-Cola being in the script.

Who do they want me to be?

Maybe I can be both.

I take a sip.

INT. ACTRESS'S BEDROOM. MORNING.

A half-finished glass of white wine sits next to a stained coffee cup on a bedside table. Posters of independent French films adorn the walls. A dressing table, make-up strewn, greetings cards and postcards emblazoned with handwritten messages -'So proud', 'I love you', 'A star!' Wilted lilies sway in the breeze from the open window.

Morning light on a lone figure wrapped in a duvet with pink hearts. A woman's hair just visible on the pillow. This is ACTRESS.

Her phone rings. Peeling the duvet from her face, she looks at the caller ID. She takes a deep breath and slaps both cheeks, hard.

>   ACTRESS
>   Phone tag! You got me!

>   AGENT
>   Finally! How you doing?

ACTRESS

I'm good, I'm great! Just getting
ready to do some — Pilates.

ACTRESS *catches sight of the half-glass
of wine. She puts her head in her hands.*

AGENT

I've been trying to touch in.

ACTRESS

Yeah, yeah, sorry. I've just been
working out a lot, getting in some
downtime.

AGENT

You must still be exhausted?

ACTRESS

No, no, I feel good, I feel great,
I'm really — good.

AGENT

People are still raving about
the play.

ACTRESS

Good. Good.

                    AGENT
We'll find you that next big thing.
OK? This year is your year, I really
believe that.

                    ACTRESS
Me too. Me too.

                    AGENT
There's a great superhero movie you'd
be amazing for, an Invisible Woman
who becomes visible in the sequel.

                    ACTRESS
Cool!

ACTRESS *takes a sip of warm wine. Coughs.*

                    ACTRESS
Sorry, just — hydrating.

                    AGENT
Then there's a Civil Rights movie,
currently untitled. I don't think
there's much in there as they're
focusing on the male leads for the
moment, but I think even without
dialogue this could be interesting.

                    ACTRESS
Wordless protest, absolutely.

                    AGENT
Exactly. Then a new TV series,
female-led, really brave.

                    ACTRESS
Women, great, always — brave.

                    AGENT
I mean, we haven't touched in for
a while, so there's a pile of
breakdowns here for you. A good
range of characters.

ACTRESS *laughs.*

                    AGENT
Sorry?

                    ACTRESS
Sorry, just, 'a pile of breakdowns'.
It's a funny — expression.

                    AGENT
Yes! Haha!

                    ACTRESS
        Break ... down ...

She rolls the words in her mouth.

                    AGENT
        Shall I go on?

                    ACTRESS
        Absolutely.

                    AGENT
        Good. There's some great love-
        interest roles, a really sexy spy —
        in a sequel for a big franchise. What
        I do have imminently is a meeting for
        a sci-fi drama — a doctor goes rogue
        in space. They're talking about it
        being a big comeback vehicle for an
        actor they won't name, he's had some
        allegations cleared, so they're going
        full steam ahead. No script yet, but
        also very exciting.

                    ACTRESS
        Who needs a script anyway!

                    AGENT
I've sent an email with the date now.
Take a look. They want you to wear
something that shows your physique —
it's an athletic role. It does also
suggest that nudity may be required,
but we can come to that should you
get it.

                   ACTRESS
An athletic doctor goes rogue on a
naked moon mission.

                    AGENT
I think you'll like this one.

ACTRESS's eyes fall on a small fly
drowning in the half-glass of wine.

                   ACTRESS
              (in a French accent)
   Super!

                    AGENT
The glass is half full.

                   ACTRESS
   Yes, it is.

                            AGENT
      This is *your* year. The perfect role
      is waiting.

ACTRESS *draws eye level with the warm*
wine, follows the small fly as it drifts
in a circle inside the glass.

                                    CUT TO:

Character: Hero, 8 yrs.
Breakdown: Afro.
Project: Commercial/TV.

Cushion on the floor, hard comb in the gentle hands of my mother, the nightly ritual of pulling the tomboy twigs from my Afro. It hurts. She forgivingly olive-oils over the damage done in the playground and an ad plays on the TV. 'Wash and Go'. A new and exclusive hair product, the first shampoo of its kind on account of it *also* being a conditioner. Two in one. I watch as a smiley brunette showers at a sports centre, applying the wonder fluid liberally. She doesn't even seem to need a towel afterwards; a glossy bob falls effortlessly down from her towel turban. The brunette's hair boings up and down in slow motion – I gasp. Her disdain for the boring everyday shampoo and conditioner the other women are using is compounded when they can't get combs through their hair after showering, it hangs lifeless on their shoulders. They need Wash and Go. I need Wash and Go. I smile. I'm sold. My prayers answered in a sexy green bottle. Less combing-hair time, more swimming, tree-climbing, Nintendo time. When I leave the pool my hair will finally fall down effortlessly rather than continue its gravity defying experiments. The brunette is so carefree as she steps out into the world. Into happiness. More time for herself. I want that. When we go to the supermarket tomorrow I'm going to buy that. Mum, I'm thankful for all your help thus far, but I'm going to manage on my own from now on. By tomorrow night you won't recognise me. I'll be shiny and new.

In the supermarket aisle, I'm on tiptoe with excitement. Every time I see something green my little heart wobbles. It's so close, this freedom, this new life where tangles and frizz and all the extra-ness on my head just flows down my back. Mum is walking quite far ahead. I don't want to be anywhere near her at the moment, frankly, as she simply isn't seeing the vision I am. She has said on multiple occasions from home, to the car, to here, that Wash and Go isn't for me. That it isn't 'right' for my hair. Well, she's shot herself in the foot already, because if they're selling it in a supermarket, it *is* for everyone. That's why they're *super*-markets, not just regular markets. Next she'll be telling me that not all toothbrushes are right for my teeth! Oh my God. There it is. It's not even stacked on a shelf like all the other tired products. It has its own green pyramid tower in between the aisles. It's a beautiful plastic Christmas tree; the fluorescent light bounces off it just so. It looks like it's alight. It's the same one, the green bottle straight from the TV. I didn't make it up in my head. It's really there and I can reach it. I'm reaching out my tiny hand and touching freedom. Everything slows down. The soft plastic gives a tiny bit in my fingers. I'm gripping it, both hands now. I want to pop the cap and lather it onto my hair immediately, see the results under the bright lights. I might cry, I feel so damn hopeful. Suddenly Mum is behind me. What is she saying? Everything is quiet in my head. What is she saying? Read her lips. 'Put.' Yes. It? 'It,' yes. 'Back.' Back? Back where? I don't want to disrupt the pyramid any more than I have to. She must mean put it in the trolley. With pleasure! She's right, lathering up here and now wouldn't be suitable. I slam-dunk it, it bounces a little on the wire, like the brunette lady's hair. What's she doing now? She's taking it out of the trolley! The world is going black and white again, backwards from the vivid Technicolor I'd temporarily been living in. Like Dorothy on rewind through Oz! No. No. No. She hasn't even put it back on its Christmas tree, she's put it on the whatever shelf with all the other no-name-whatever shit.

'It's not right for your hair, Zawe, please believe me.'

The words ring out clear and my feelings are hurt. I'm crying, instantly. The crying that hurts the middle of your chest. I pull at Mum, I pull at my own hair. Mum looks scared. I'm scared too, because of how much I want this. I'm now trying to physically shake my hair from my head. Side to side, backwards and forwards. I am a tree shaking its roots to shed its dead leaves. I'm serious. I want it gone. I want to be in control of my *hair*. I'm moshing in the cosmetic aisle of Safeway because

even though I'm only eight I find my hair so stress-
ful it makes me want to punch out at the air until I'm
sick. Tress stress. Has Mum thought about the next
eight years of my life? Has she thought about how as I
become bigger, *it* will become bigger. What if it outgrows
me altogether and picks up in the wind like a hot-air
balloon? Has Mum thought about *that*? Shake shake
shake shake shake shake shake shake shake shake shake
shake shake shake, punch punch punch punch punch
punch punch punch punch, kick kick kick kick kick kick
kick kick kick kick kick –

'Excuse me, madam, is this your child? Please control her.'

If there's one thing Mum hates, it's when I temper-
tantrum in public and people look sideways at us. The
attention from the store representative makes her return
the green bottle to the bottom of the trolley. Ha! Seriously, thank God for that woman. I wave at her, smiling,
until she turns the corner at the toilet roll. There it is.
For keeps. My heart is a paper aeroplane.

I know how to lock the bathroom door. Easy. I know
how to run the bath taps. Easy. I've clocked how the
grown-ups do it, not a problem. What I'm *not* actually
sure I know how to do is wash my own hair. That's
always taken care of while my eyes are squeezed tight.
How hard can it be? I lock the door, run the taps and flip
the cap on the bottle with my thumbs. I am *handling* this.
I could be twenty-five.

The wonder stuff comes out so pearly white and smells so fresh, I'm giddy. This purifying liquid is going to silky-smooth me, I feel it. Put some in the front. That's good. Rub it in. Some in the back. Make hands into a little bucket shape and mix some water in, that's working. Bubbles! Yes, it's definitely working. Repeat, repeat, splash water, repeat. Stick head under the tap. Don't admit how much your eyes are stinging. Don't call for help. They'll try and take it from you again. This is freedom.

It's working. It's working. I can feel it, under my fingers, my hair unlocking! It will soon be glossy enough to swish in my parents' faces. Everyone who makes fun of me at school? The gloss will blind them all!

I drip my head out of the bath onto my swimming towel, which I had put carefully in place earlier. I wrap it around my head, rubbing my hair like I'm waiting for a genie. When it feels as dry as the lady in the advert made hers, I open my eyes. Step up on the toilet, draw level with the mirror. I untwist the orca-print towel from my tiny head. It falls past the toilet to the floor, eating its own tail. I stare at my reflection. I move my head left, then right. I walk round on myself – craning my neck as best I can to see the back of my head. What's gone wrong? This isn't a bob, this isn't gloss that can blind adults and children alike? This is just my old hair but – worse? It's all off to one side. It's not even curls any more, it's dark brown candyfloss. I'm going to tap it with my palm. When the brunette touched her hair

20

like this, it bounced back and tumbled down. My hand reaches up. I feel how brittle it really is and it takes me aback. There's a sudden knock at the door. An urgent knock. Look at this mess. I don't want to give up. The knocking keeps coming. Then a shout. Can we all just *keep calm*? Maybe they think I'm drowning myself. Oops, yeah, left the tap on. I'm not sure how much time has passed. The sounds in the room are magnified in my hot ears. The rising water in the bath sounds like a violent storm over the sea. The banging on the door is a woodcutter splintering wood. I have to be bigger than the noises, they're distracting me! I have to do something before the door splits and the whole world shatters. Because if I'm wrong and the TV lies and Mum has to comb my hair until I'm twenty, my heart will break. My eye catches something sparkling behind me in the mirror. The whole room is vibrating now. The sparkly thing looks like Tinkerbell hovering up and down in the glass. Calling me over. Oh, I see, yes, I see you. I see you, shiny fairy wings. I see you – scissors.

Once they're wrapped round my fingers, the room is quiet again, the sea in the bathtub laps lazily now instead of raging. The insistent knocking is just a soundtrack to my triumph.

Snip. Little slip. Snip. Handful of tough curl. Snip. One more fistful. Snip! The dead hair floats to the ground. One more snip. Door opens. Oh dear. Close eyes. Open one. Mum's had to bust the lock. She's not going to like that. I don't need to look back though, this new style feels pretty certain on my head. I can sort of sense it's good. Not quite down-the-back flowing, but it feels – different. I look up at Mum; Dad isn't far behind, dashing for scissors, running taps and waterlogged floor. He looks like a frightened octopus. Mum? I communicate with expectant eyes and sweet smile alone. Is it a glossy bob? Hopeful eyes widen. Is this front bit of hair I can feel about to relax into a fringe? My ticket to same-ness? I'm not getting much hopeful eye contact back. Better turn to the mirror for the facts.

Little.

Heart.

Break.

It's a breeze block.

It's a rectangle where the effortless fringe should be and a square everywhere else. This isn't a glossy bob. Staring into this mirror is the equivalent of being told Santa doesn't exist. It's one of the first times I've been in control of how I look. It's one of the first times I'm aware of how I look impacting on how I feel. About myself. The hot tears start to prick behind my eyes as it dawns on me, it's school the next day. I was supposed to blind them with my bone-straight hair. Instead I'll blind them with a hair javelin to the face.

Mum scoops me up. Will they still love me looking like this? Do they even recognise me as theirs? Mum gets to work on softening some of the edges. Her gentle hands smooth out the hurt. She was right.

When the TV talks about hair, it hasn't got round to talking about me.

'Will I ever be able to wash and go?'

'Don't move your head, sweetheart.'

Dad's breathing like he's been fighting, two wet patches on his work trousers. I expect a punishment, but he says I can play Nintendo. I jump to my feet. I need to become a hair invalid more often! Before I grab the control pad, Dad and Mum both sink down to my height. They hold my hands, stroke hair tufts, say they were worried. Say they love my hair. Say I must always be myself. Blah blah blah! Someone get the remote! The TV fizzes to life. The end of an ad plays out, a new one. A blonde woman smiles and washes her hair in a stream. The light bounces off it as she stares down the lens, content, the water running clear over the clean yellow strands. A *stream*? I'm not falling for it this time. She looks happy, sure, carefree, but she's got to get up early and wash her hair *outside*? I'm not buying your lies any more, television. Maybe the brunette never even used Wash and Go. Maybe she was actually wearing a wig! No one's hair dries that goddamn fast. Nintendo case click, remote click, TV fizz to video mode, then black. And there's me. I can see myself. I'm in the TV. I can see where Mum's put the hair that's still long enough into plaits. Glitter hairbands restrain all they can. The fringe is still a wedge despite multiple oil manipulations. It's 3D before there was 3D. It's ahead of its time, this fringe. For all its progressiveness, it won't stop school being

23

bad tomorrow. But then I see Mum and Dad, reflections behind me. Supporting cast. They're worried. They look more like little kids than me. Look at us three. This feels real, in here. Not like the TV.

INT. AUDITION ROOM, WEST LONDON. MORNING.

CASTING DIRECTOR *adjusts the camera.*
ACTRESS *stands in a T-shirt and ill-
fitting leggings. ACTRESS strokes her
hair, shakes her hands out by her
sides.*

                    CASTING DIRECTOR
          Your bod looks great, your arms.

                    ACTRESS
          Thanks. I've been working out.

                    CASTING DIRECTOR
          Do you have a change of clothes?
          Before we start?

                    ACTRESS
          This is, it said -

                    CASTING DIRECTOR
          The notes say 'figure-hugging'
          I think?

                    ACTRESS
          Oh, yeah, well, I can tie this —

She pulls aimlessly at her baggy T-shirt.

                    CASTING DIRECTOR
We need to *see* you, they need to be
able to see you.

                         ACTRESS
See me?

                    CASTING DIRECTOR
Producers, the director, they're
tired, they want to be able to
go — yep, there's our girl.

                         ACTRESS
Sure.

                    CASTING DIRECTOR
Before you've opened your mouth.

                         ACTRESS
They need my body to talk.

                    CASTING DIRECTOR
I really like you, I want them to
like you. I thought your play was
fantastic. You were mesmerising.

                         ACTRESS
Thank you. It's anxiety. I think. The
arms? I'm ripped!

CASTING DIRECTOR *looks concerned for a moment.*

                    ACTRESS
        Maybe -

ACTRESS *ties her T-shirt in a knot at the back. We see the outline of her waist.*

                CASTING DIRECTOR
        Maybe just, a little more to the —

CASTING DIRECTOR *gestures.*

                    ACTRESS
        Oh, yeah.

ACTRESS *pulls the knot in her T-shirt until it shows her belly.*

                CASTING DIRECTOR
        Cool!

                    ACTRESS
        Isn't she a biophysicist?

                CASTING DIRECTOR
        Happy to go for one?

ACTRESS *nods*.

          CASTING DIRECTOR
  'Hey, people are dropping like flies
  out here.'

          ACTRESS
  'Don't worry, I've completed work on
  the vaccine.'

          CASTING DIRECTOR
  'The vaccine to save our species?'

          ACTRESS
  'Yes. Maybe even the entire galaxy.
  Cancers, deficiencies, contagions of
  any kind will be wiped out with a
  single drop of *this*.'

*She bends down, then holds up a tiny
carton of apple juice.*

          CASTING DIRECTOR
  'One elixir to save us all, just as
  the Cryonauts predicted.'

          ACTRESS
  'Yes. But my research had to be
  quick, the physics and my theories

have been rushed. To *save* our lives,
we will need to *risk* our lives.'

*She takes the straw on the side of the
carton and plunges it into the silver
seal. A drip of juice emerges.*

ACTRESS
'Do you trust me?'

CASTING DIRECTOR
'I trust you with my life, Professor
Kollins.'

ACTRESS *awkwardly turns her forearm
towards the camera.*

CASTING DIRECTOR
'Oh my God, your arm? What happened
to your arm?'

ACTRESS
'I had to experiment on myself.'

*She brings the carton towards her
ominously.*

ACTRESS
'We have lift-off.'

She takes the straw in her lips and takes a sip. We see the light brown liquid travel up the straw. She swallows.

ACTRESS
'Argh! Argh! Argh! Nooooo!'

She starts to claw at her face, her skin.

ACTRESS
'Argh! My skin! It's burning! My organs! It's eating me! It's eating me *alive*!!!'

CASTING DIRECTOR
'Professor! Professor! Damn those Cryonauts to hell!'

ACTRESS, *still miming wildly, slips and falls to the floor, the carton falls and spills.*

ACTRESS
Ow! Sorry!

CASTING DIRECTOR
You OK?

ACTRESS *gets to her feet.*

                    ACTRESS
          Life imitating art!

She smiles, rubbing her arm.

                 CASTING DIRECTOR
          I can cut that out. Can you say
          your height?

                    ACTRESS
          Five foot ten.

                 CASTING DIRECTOR
          And how do you keep fit?

                    ACTRESS
          Mixed . . . martial . . . arts.

                 CASTING DIRECTOR
          Turn to your left and right for
          profiles.

*ACTRESS turns left, pauses, and we see
her profile in full. She turns right and
we see her profile in full. She turns
back and stares down the lens.*

                 CASTING DIRECTOR
          And your name, please.

                      31

                    ACTRESS
Professor Kollins.

                CASTING DIRECTOR
Your name, sorry.

                    ACTRESS
Professor Kollins.

                                        CUT TO:

```
Character: Young Cowboy, 9 yrs+.
Breakdown: Blond preferable.
Project: Commercial/TV.
```

Our drama teacher stops class early to gather us for some news.

There's a nationwide search to find a new Milky Bar Kid.

The room bursts with whispers. Apparently the campaign is tired and needs a shake-up, the kid they've got is running low on relevance. The current ad depicts him as a cowboy in a Western shoot-out. He rides into town on a Shetland pony at dusk, his hat low over his eyes. His nemesis, the Sheriff, opens a Milky Bar and chews it nonchalantly outside the saloon. Any lackadaisical treatment of his bars is a trigger for the Kid – he lassoes a barrel of treacle at twelve paces and tars and feathers the Sherriff on the spot. To the town's delight, not only has he saved them from a dastardly overlord, he's here to dole out Milky Bars – *and* they're on *him*! He distributes them freely among the down-and-outs and dancing girls, cue catchy theme tune with its message about the creamiest milk making the whitest bars and only the best being good enough.

I need to be at that open call.

I can make up a Milky Bar Kid break-dance.

I can rap the theme tune. They'd be lucky to have my individual talents as part of their brand strategy. If fresh is what they want, here I am.

I put my hand in the air and wave until it hurts, I need the details *now*, I want to put my name down *now*, I need Mum to take me – *now*. Ten other kids have the same idea; we suck the air from our cheeks until they burn.

Our drama teacher waves a hand. The story isn't over.

'Yesterday, on the first day of the open call, a young boy was turned away, without an audition. Because he was black.'

We all lower our hands.

'He arrived at the front of the queue and was told he couldn't possibly be the Milky Bar Kid, because of the colour of his skin. He left without being seen.'

He left without being seen.

My brain is skipping.

'We're going to take the rest of the class to discuss this. Get into pairs.'

As my teacher speaks, all I can see is a little boy made of chocolate, melting.

What did his mum say? Were his whole family with him? What did *they* say? How did he leave the room? How long was the line outside? Which way was the exit? Did they have to walk past the queue? Was everyone blond? Did he have to notify every other black child he saw? Was he the only one? How long had *he* waited? Did anyone leave with him, once they heard?

The thoughts come so fast. I can *see* him. I can feel him.

Maybe he was going to put his own twist on the theme tune too. Like I would have. That's what they wanted, wasn't it?

A modern take on an original?

How long did he have to stand there?

How long did he have to stand there waiting for them to explain just how they see the colour of milk?

INT. ACTRESS'S BEDROOM. LATE AFTERNOON.

ACTRESS *lies face down on the bed, she wears a full-length vintage gown made of sequins, unzipped; her feet are bare. There are remnants of pain au chocolat on the bedside table.*

The phone rings and rings and rings. Without lifting her head, ACTRESS walks her fingers slowly towards it like two tired legs. It goes to voicemail.

ACTRESS *turns her head, cheek squashed against the duvet, she stares at the phone.*

We hear voice-over, ACTRESS's voice, perky and professional.

> ACTRESS (*v.o.*)
> Hi, I'm sorry I'm not around right now. I look forward to picking up your message. You know what to do after that beep!

The beep.

AGENT (*v.o.*)

Me again! You're probably at
Pilates, but give me a call —
checking you've got my message
and the email with details about
the screen test. You must have
nailed it for them to come back
so quickly with a test. They are
dying to see you again!

ACTRESS
(*to herself*)

But — I fell over?

AGENT (*v.o.*)

Whatever you did, you nailed it!
They are SO into you. Feedback
was that clothes could have been
a little more flattering, I think
you discussed that, something
more to the body this time maybe.
Doesn't have to be a catsuit!
This would be a game-changer. Let me
know when you've got this. You can
ignore the message about the all-
female Shakespeare, they've gone
older. Bye!

ACTRESS *slides onto her back; her chest rises and falls. She takes deep breaths. The sequins come alive in the early-evening sun, erratic circles dance across the ceiling above her.*

                                    CUT TO:

Character: Honeysuckle, 8–12 yrs.
Breakdown: Sweet as a summer flower.
Project: Musical/regional theatre.
Notes from casting: Cute girls who MUST
BE ABLE TO SING/DANCE/MOVE.

I can't stop touching the pink leotard on my skin.

I pet my own body. I pet my non-existent breasts under the shiny Lycra.

The girls in pink are flowers and the girls in green are herbs. We all sing together in a magical garden. An evil witch captures a princess in a tower and the all-singing, all-dancing magical flowers and herbs in the garden below help to break the spell.

Even *we* know it's dreadful. As kids we can instinctively pick up on the whiff of desperation that follows the grown-ups involved in the show. When they come to rehearsals, they don't even clap any more. They spend most of their time huddled in groups, rubbing their foreheads. But it's all worth it, because of this costume. I've got a safety raft in this sinking ship of a musical and it's made of pink spandex. The girls in green are constantly crying because their herb costumes itch. They have to wear thick green woollen tights under felt shorts and brown shoes made of old sacks, with toes that curl up at the end. They look like the elves Santa forgot. Even their *hats* are itchy! I touched one. Like a shaved cat. They've got to wear belts with little pockets, containing really smelly herbs. It's the putting on of the belts that gets the tears going – it makes the outfit inescapable. I like to see them cry. It makes me feel even more free.

I'm playing 'Honeysuckle', the sweetest of all the flowers in the garden. I'm pink, like pink soda! My tutu is pink like the pink wafers your grandma gives you – it floats me on a pink cloud. My hat isn't itchy. It's the accessory to end all accessories. It's made of silk petals. It's like a huge flower bell hung on your head and it rings. I feel drunk with its nectar! I can actually *smell* flowers in here! I am *in* a garden. I *am* a honeysuckle, not a gangly prepubescent, I'm a *flower*. There's no shape I feel embarrassed to strike. The herb girls say they feel like their costumes are for boys and ours are for girls. But when I'm dancing, I could burst. I don't feel like a *girl*. I feel – genuinely – like a *flower*.

One of the girls lives near me. We ride together to and from rehearsals. She's quiet and polite and we eat sweets and play I Spy. One day, she gets in the car and starts kicking the passenger seat in front of her.

'I don't want to do it any more!' she yells. 'It's not fair!' She calls out to my dad: 'I don't want to be a herb! I don't want to be a herb! I want to be a flower! They made me look like a BOY!'

She could have been screaming: 'Don't operate on my brain!'

There's a pain in her voice that makes me look out of the window and pretend I'm not there.

I let her get out of the car without saying goodbye and she screams for her mum at the front door. Dad is concerned.

'Do you want to stop too? You can stop any time you want. This is your choice.'

But I don't want to stop.

'I want to be a flower for as long as I can.'

When we pick her up the next day, she gets in the car with a silence not normal for a kid. It fills everything up. At the theatre, putting on my costume feels like putting on a wet swimsuit. Before, being inside the flower hat was like wearing pink air and taking drugged honey. Now it feels damp and nasty and hangs on my body totally differently from before. I try to help my friend when I see her putting on her costume like it's poison ivy. I try to cheer her up. I point at one of the other flower girls.

'She's got hairy arms,' I whisper. 'She looks more like a boy than you.'

As soon as I say it, I get a stomach ache.

'What did you say?'

The girl with the hairy arms clearly has supersonic hearing.

'Nothing.'

'She said you've got hairy arms,' one of the herb girls chimes in.

This girl whose lip is now quivering, who I'm shaming for having hair on her arms, is my friend. She helps me with my dance steps all the time. I look around; all these girls have become friends this summer.

Another herb jumps to her defence.

'*You* need a training bra.'

'And sometimes you smell.'

I'm nearly outnumbered now.

'Shut up, you're the ones who look like smelly boys!'

My flower girls have got my back, but I don't want this.

'Just leave it, yeah?' says my herb friend I was trying to cheer up. 'Stop acting like kids.'

She sounds like one of the grown-ups. Those adults have divided us. Made us as disappointed and incomplete as them.

My flower hat droops.

Just before opening night, I'm 'invited' to the costume department by the designer. She wants to talk to me, about my leotard. I'm glad. Despite the bad atmosphere, it's still my favourite subject. It'll be nice to get away for a while.

The costume department is a warehouse-sized wardrobe. Clothes hover in every inch of space. I stand on a small block, arms raised as the designer wraps her tape measure round me.

'I think it might be a growth spurt. We might have to get you a leotard from the adult department. They have a little bit of a built-in cup.'

When she says 'cup' she doesn't make a drinking gesture; instead she takes both her index fingers and runs them underneath her boobs. Her adult boobs. Her very <u>existent</u> breasts.

'I like my costume as it is.'

She brings a small cellophane package noisily out of a drawer.

The adult-sized leotards are quite different to the kids'. They're a softer pink, the material is thicker and slightly ribbed. Not shiny like my old one. The sleeves go down to my elbows. I don't like this. Marks me out as different to the others. My arms look too long.

On opening night, we have a group hug backstage, our arms limply holding each other's waists. The curtain goes up. The herbs have an intro dance number. There's a spontaneous – round of applause? By the first musical number, people are heckling from the stalls. The herbs are getting all the laughs! The herb lines are edgy, peppered with great jokes and us flowers are drowning in wet one-liners. We don't actually *do* anything! The herbs get to run around the stage spouting lines that seem to have been redrafted by an Oscar-winning writer overnight. We just sit there in our flower pots and react. *And* our flower hats keep falling down over our faces! I feel pink and useless. My new adult-length sleeves are holding me back.

After an hour and a half, the magical garden feels more like an overgrown cemetery. At the curtain call, the girls who have been human cacti for a month put their hands on their belts – triumphant – and throw herbs from their itchy pouches in to the audience! They stand with their feet astride and bow – like Peter Pan bidding farewell to Neverland. I hide behind the petals attached to my head which now smell less like honey and more like adult sweat as my chest throbs against the elastic.

In the wings my flower friend takes my shoulders and presses her hat against mine; we lock each other in a horrified gaze. She takes my hand for the second bow, grips it to the bone. I look down. As we skip back towards the stage I can see back under the lights, that she's attempted to shave one of her arms.

INT. ACTRESS'S BEDROOM. DAY.

ACTRESS, *in pyjamas, lies in bed.* MOTHER
stands at the foot of the bed.

> MOTHER
> You're not a child any more.

> ACTRESS
> I know.

> MOTHER
> Even as a newborn you embraced
> the dramatic. It was one of the
> longest labours ever recorded on
> the ward.

> ACTRESS
> I know.

> MOTHER
> Then when everyone was exhausted
> and they said you'd have to be
> a C-section, you finally made an
> appearance.

> ACTRESS
> Really?

                    MOTHER
A grand entrance!

                    ACTRESS
I'm sure it wasn't deliberate.

                    MOTHER
Kept your audience waiting.

                    ACTRESS
Huh.

                    MOTHER
It worked. Even the midwife was
completely in love with you.
Captivated.

                    ACTRESS
I would have preferred to stay in
there.

                    MOTHER
Then it was another drama when
you couldn't fit in the cot. Too
tall!

                    ACTRESS
Hardly my fault!

MOTHER

When are you going to get out of this
bed? Have a shower?

ACTRESS

I went out this morning!

MOTHER

You went out, got changed back into
pyjamas and got back into bed?

ACTRESS

I was walking briskly, I needed a
lie-down.

MOTHER *opens the blinds. Opens the
window a crack.* ACTRESS *shields her
eyes, like a vampire, against the light.*

ACTRESS

Argh!

MOTHER

I leave you messages, you don't get
back.

ACTRESS

I'm fine.

                         MOTHER
You can't kid a kidder.

                        ACTRESS
Are we in a film from the forties?

                         MOTHER
There's an empty bottle of wine under
the bed.

                        ACTRESS
Is there? I think that was there when
I moved in.

                         MOTHER
We're worried.

                        ACTRESS
I'm *OK*. I'm just, I suppose,
I'm just hiding.

                         MOTHER
From what?

                        ACTRESS
I keep feeling like . . .
people are . . . looking at me . . .

MOTHER

Someone's looking at you? Through the
curtains? What? Have you told the
police?

MOTHER *goes to the curtains and closes
them again.*

ACTRESS

No! Not like that! Don't you ever
feel eyes on you?

MOTHER

You can come home to me and your dad
for a while.

ACTRESS

That's not necessary.

MOTHER

Something's gone seriously wrong.

ACTRESS

I've stayed in bed a couple of days,
weeks, whatever — it's fine.

MOTHER

Where did I go wrong?

                    ACTRESS
        Mum, this isn't about *you*, this
        is about *me*. And *I* am better
        than ever!

ACTRESS *punches the air wildly, an*
attempt at genuine excitement. It
tires her out. The two women look at
each other. MOTHER *rifles in her bag,*
produces a lip gloss.

                    MOTHER
        This was on sale, it doesn't look
        good on me.

She hands it to ACTRESS.

                    MOTHER
        Put a little bit on.

ACTRESS *stares at it.*

                    MOTHER
        You'll feel better.

                    ACTRESS
        Make-up doesn't solve things.

                    MOTHER
Where's your hairbrush?

                    ACTRESS
Hair definitely doesn't solve things.

                    MOTHER
I'll do it.

MOTHER *sits and unscrews the lip gloss.*
Approaches ACTRESS, *who squints. Just*
before it touches her lips, ACTRESS
covers her face with the duvet.

                    ACTRESS
No, no, no!

                    MOTHER
What's this all about?

                    ACTRESS
I don't know, I don't know. Who's it
all for?

                    MOTHER
You want to stay in bed for the rest
of your days?

ACTRESS
(*suddenly hopeful, she removes duvet*)
Do you think I could?

MOTHER
Your grandmother is nearing ninety
and doesn't go anywhere without a
little something on. Her handbag.

ACTRESS
Do you think *she* ever gets tired?

CUT TO:

```
Character: Zara, 11+ yrs.
Breakdown: Tall, ethnically ambiguous
best friend.
Project: High school dramedy/feature.
```

The first day at a new school and the general girl rage is
already aimed at my head.

The first bonding exercise and I'm that kid.

I'm that kid that hasn't judged the room.

Girls of the pre-teen variety shift nervously from
foot to foot at the front of the class, twist their braids or
the corner of their skirts or circle their fists inside their
sleeves as they name their favourite foods, sports and
music. I'm near the top of the roll call. Stupid surname.
My Bambi legs carry me up to the front and I tower
over the teacher as she conducts the random inquest.
I'm already spooked because the twelve-hole Doc Martens I've decided to match with my uniform have been
attracting disapproving side eyes since I walked in the
gates. I'm so fucking nervous, I can't remember any of
the reasons why I like bolognese. I play the first questions
safe, direct my answers at the loners, the English-as-
a-second-language crew and any of the girls with new-
ly fitted braces. I'm specifically avoiding the excitable
group at the back who are letting their impressive snore
sound effects get more and more powerful. The teacher
makes the mistake of being intimidated and I make the
mistake of carrying on. She asks me what music I like.

It's the easiest question so far, in fact it makes me smile
to answer, because the bands I like are my tribe colours.
Along with my Doc Martens, they stand with me. I can
fly back to my seat on this one.

'Blur,' says me.

And the out-of-body experience begins. Wrong.
Crowd. The laughter erupts. It's not even laughter, it's
just sort of a continuous –

'AAAEEEEEEERRRRRR???!!!'

Even the non-English-speaking contingent are
happy to have a moment of release. They're now talking
animatedly among themselves. Every single girl lets
something out. Even the anaemic ill-advised-novelty-
hair-clip group. I was relying on them. The excited
back-row girls have gone into overdrive, grabbing
at each other as though they're old women having
strokes, heart attacks, from the shock of – me. I've
brought them together as fast friends with my massive
goof. I have one mate, one mate who I was at primary school with. She's in the front row. She sits quietly,
staring ahead. She's my little mate, I've known her
since we were eight, she wears Doc Martens too, but
her feet are smaller than mine. She can't afford to know
me now.

My band choice doesn't say 'cool' to this lot, it marks
me out as having an affinity with men who have long
hair and don't wash. Who sing out of tune on purpose
and are so skinny they look like young girls jumping
around and staring, indifferently, down the barrel of

MTV. They aren't oiled and ripped, don't shop at Gap. They're more Oxfam. More dingy. More other.

The second irreversible gaffe is out of my control. I'm going to be on TV. I am going to be in a children's television programme, tonight. After school, my face will be in their living rooms. Do they sell bullet-proof vests in Woolworths?

The next morning, my boots fall heavy on the pavement. Small sounds make me jump. Walk into class, draw blood with my fingernails inside my hand, wait for the firing squad. Instead, I find my anti-advocates – *smiling* in my direction? Did TV change their minds about me? I choose the seat by the open window with the five-storey drop, just in case.

'Hey, giiiiirrrrlll!'

The leader of the anti-me campaign has her arm gently round my shoulder. She smells of crisps. I always imagined her breath to smell like a mixture of cigarette smoke and blood. But she smells like a kid. Like me.

'Good performance last night, you know?'

The rest of her hate campaigners join in with a protracted –

'Yeeeeeahhhh.'

My head is exploding for real. Clips of detonated buildings and swelling dust clouds flash inside my brain as the two frontal lobes tear apart.

'I didn't watch it, but – thanks.'

I *did* watch it, my whole family were round the TV, watching the story of an evil headmaster unfold. Last night his least faithful minions were exterminated in a secret lab. I was the one who wouldn't give up without a fight.

'Why don't you come and sit with us?'

My frontal lobe disintegrates completely. I get up slowly from my chair, drag my bag to the back of class. As I wade into the murky water, my little friend, the one from primary school, walks in. She manages to flick her eyes over without being clocked. She's got brand-new Hush Puppies on her feet.

'You see that bit where you were screaming and they had to pull you in the lift?' says Princess Pain.

Oh God, she watched all the way to the end.

'Did they do that for real? Was that boy allowed to pull you like that?'

'It's just fake. There's someone who tells you how to do it.'

'That bit was good, the way you were screaming it was like, good, it looked real.'

'Thanks.'

'You love acting, yeah?'

'No.'

'You like being on TV?'

'No.'

'So, what? Someone *makes* you do it?'

'No. I just do it.'

'You like people watching you, yeah?'

'No.'

'Get me on TV.'

'I dunno.'

'You don't think I could do it? Pretend all that shit? I could do it better than you!'

'I know you could, I'm shit at it. No, I just, it's just – the filming's finished now. We filmed that last year.'

'*Filming*, you know. *Listen* to *her*.'

In the lunch hall, Team Aggravation show me off like a prize to anyone who looks our way.

'*Yes*, she was on telly! You wanna ask her something?'

It feels like being made of pure power, just floating in their shoal. I see others like me, like I was before today, cowering as we approach. We used to blend into the walls together. I walk down the centre of the hallway now. They pull me like a stuffed doll.

'Make way for the actress!'

They take both my wrists and wave them above my head like a coach would a prizefighter. My armpits tingle with fear and joy.

'This girl's famous, y'know! Move!'

They shout on my behalf as we all cut the lunch line, leaving hungry bodies in our wake.

'Miss, Miss, you should give us more chips! Our friend was on telly last night!'

The dinner lady looks at me straight.

'You the friend?'

If I had any frontal lobe left I might nod. Did they just call me *friend*?

'Yeah!'

They bomb me with one-arm hugs. Dinner lady takes a deep breath and shovels more chips into my polystyrene box. She's a woman with no love left, her hands move like an old snake. She doesn't even blink when chips shower out of the box, onto the floor. The She-Wolf Gang all scream at once at the sight of the overflowing pot of crispy gold.

'Actually, all of us were! All of us were! We were all on TV! Miss! Miss!!!!!!'

Another few bone-weary shovels and chips are flowing like dimes from a jackpot. Have I somehow become friends with these girls? Is this my new – home? Reigning terror over the weedlings doesn't feel like a role I'm cut out for, but it's worth it for free chips and an aggro-free hall pass. We walk slow-motion across the playground, we're hard as the concrete. My little friend from primary school sits a way off, eating chicken nuggets.

'I hate that girl, you know.'

They point straight at her, blatant and clear.

'Are you friends with her?'

'No! I hardly know her.'

Just like that, my childhood is erased.

'You wear the same boots though? They look like a farmer's shoes.'

'Yeah, I'm not gonna wear these any more.'

'You gonna get us on telly though, yeah?'

'Yeah.'

Shoulder shrug. I harden my face into a scowl and manage to sit with these girls all day. Crisps, Coke, laughs, no hair yanks or bruises from sly hallway knocks. Yes, it feels like treading water, constantly, and I still flinch when they comedy high-five me, but my stupid face on the TV has redressed the power play, it's reordered the food chain! I've gone from Library Dweller to Canteen Princess in the space of a day. During class, our English teacher asks what's got into me; I throw a scrunched-up crisp packet at her head when she turns to the whiteboard. When the bell goes, I join in with the exaggerated body rolls and whoops of my new clan. I've studied the ecstatic behaviour of this tribe from behind exercise books and strategically placed graph paper. I can assimilate.

We're nearly out of the door, arms around each other, when I get a tap on the shoulder. Teacher wants a word. Oh my GOD. The door closes and my new friends dance, upbeat, down the corridor and away without looking back. I'm not sure they've noticed I'm gone. They kick the double doors open and their shapes drown out in light.

'I'll catch you up!' I shout through the glass.

Teacher sits me down and there's this wobble in her voice, more than usual. Now that I'm powerful, I can see how truly weak she is. Her teeth are tobacco-stained and there's a tan line where her wedding ring was.

Weak. She's the one sinking, not me. She trembles when she calls the fucking register! Occasionally she makes a good point about the Romantic poets, but my one day of acting bored and distracted has made me realise how little I care about schoolwork at all.

'I've found something which I think you should know about.'

'I didn't do nothing.'

This is my favourite role to date.

'I'd like us to go and see the Head, together, right now.'

The character slips, my back pulls me straight, feet turned in toe to toe, mortal adolescent once more.

'Why?'

'I found something, in the bin. A note. A note that was going round class, which I'm glad I intercepted.'

Good word.

'I didn't pass a note, I swear, I was doing my work.'

'I know you didn't write it. It was written *about* you.'

'Oh.'

'The girls you were sat with.'

She lists them by name with a weariness that makes her eyes roll back in her head and stay there.

'They're my friends. Can I see it?'

'Get your bag, let's go.'

I don't get it. I was included in everything today. Tippexing over pictures of historical figures in textbooks, kicking empty cans over the fence, punching the work chosen to be displayed on the stairwell. If there was a note, I would have known about it.

The Head Teacher has a perm that is hard to take seriously. Her face has a perpetual redness, which I can now see up close is caused by erratic red and purple veins that meander all over her cheeks. She asks me to sit down. Miss Weakheart sits in the corner.

'You're very lucky that this was found today. I don't want you to be afraid, this is quite normal for first-year pupils.'

'What does it say? I don't understand what's going on.'

She reads. It's excruciating, she imitates the individual voices of the Hate Crew in a generic patois lilt that makes my entire spine wince.

'This girl think she – too nice.

'But she so fuckin ugly.

'I know.

'Ooooh – she ugly.

'She looked so fuckin ugly on the TV. She gonna try walk home with us, ya know. She can't walk wid us on road wi dem boots.'

I'm not sure why she doesn't just let me read this to myself. This isn't the moment to practise accents for her amateur dramatics class. How did they write this without me seeing? Had I accidentally done some work while they weren't watching? It goes on for a while. How ugly I am. How up myself. How pathetic. Then there's a detailed plan of how to jump me at the back gates. How to get me alone and then beat me. Until my face is unrecognisable.

Now she hands it to me to read; her hands are shaking and she's embarrassed. She can't act any more. I can. I read the writing at the end which has been scrawled over.

It says:

'Don't stop. Even if she looks dead.'

It feels like my nose is about to bleed from fear, but I shrug my shoulders and look both women square in the eye.

Mum has to come and get me. They can't send me home alone. I sit and stare at the motivational quote posters for young women.

'Young women, young futures.'

'I am strong, I am worthy, I am beautiful.'

'Be yourself, everyone else is taken.'

I don't want to be anyone.

On the car ride home, I decide to stop acting, for ever. Nothing good comes of being visible. I have to watch my back, and learn to walk in new shoes.

INT. 24-HOUR OFF-LICENCE, HIGH STREET.
NIGHT.

ACTRESS *takes two bottles of discounted
wine to the* SHOPKEEPER. *They clearly
have history.*

> SHOPKEEPER
> How are you? You fine? This is nice
> wine.

> ACTRESS
> It is. Yeah, looks really good,
> inside the bottle.

> SHOPKEEPER
> You big girl now, isn't it?
> Big girls can buy wine.

> ACTRESS
> How's your lovely wife?

> SHOPKEEPER
> Same, same. I tell you always, you
> can be my other wife.

> ACTRESS
> You do always tell me that.

                    SHOPKEEPER
For years!

                     ACTRESS
Since I was very young, yes.

                    SHOPKEEPER
I see you look at me.

                     ACTRESS
Sometimes you're standing in front of
the wine.

                    SHOPKEEPER
In my country you couldn't do this.
Walk on the street with alcohol.

                     ACTRESS
It's a privilege. Buy one get one
half price, yeah?

                    SHOPKEEPER
Walk in the street with the pyjama!

Pause.

                     ACTRESS
These aren't pyjamas.

                    SHOPKEEPER
Slipper.

                     ACTRESS
... Nope.

                    SHOPKEEPER
They lock you up!

                                        CUT TO:

```
Character: Charlene, 14 yrs.
Breakdown: Love interest of notorious
gang leader. Supporting role.
Project: Award-winning police drama.
Notes from casting: Need a young actress
who won't 'disappear' in gang of men.
```

I've never kissed anyone. My first kiss is scheduled in an hour. At work.

As the girlfriend of a gang leader, I have to keep the secret of his whereabouts. But when we're caught kissing on some CCTV footage, his cover's blown. I get off with a caution, but he goes down for life.

In my trailer I kiss the back of my hand. Move my lips up and down and around, the way I've seen in the films. I let my tongue slip in and out of the space between my thumb and first finger. I don't know that this is going to feel good on someone's face. Counting down the minutes, I wipe the drool on the back of my leg and spit a snowball of chewing gum in the bin.

One more douse of vanilla body spray under the armpits, a short blast in a circle round the crotch. It's cold and stings and makes me walk funny. Why have I chosen this moment as the *first time ever* to spray my *crotch*? I scratch myself as discreetly as possible on the long walk to the location.

*

There he is. My saliva sparring partner. He's older than me. He holds his hand out to shake.

'You smell nice.'

My cheeks and crotch are on fire. I smile and look out across the estate we're shooting on.

I want to ask how many people he's kissed before, but I don't. Instead I end up telling him I live nearby. I don't. Our small talk is taken up by me outlining a detailed imaginary map of the route to my house from where we stand.

When the director appears he doesn't introduce himself, just puts his hands on the back of our heads and pushes us nose to nose for the camera. Only, his nose comes more to my chin.

'How tall *are* you?' The director asks.

'Um?'

When you play girlfriends people just assume you're petite, I don't know why. Leading men are almost always short, so you'd think the people in casting would double-check your dimensions before giving you the job.

'You're a giant.'

He says it with a smile but my crotch is on fire with embarrassment. The director whispers something to the camera assistant who runs off like a messenger with bad news. The director comes close to me, exhaling his coffee breath and scaling me with his eyes like you would a rare tree in the Amazon. I start to feel sick. The assistant comes back with a wooden box.

'For you.'

He nods at my leading man. Is this for him to *stand on*? He has to stand on a box to make me look normal? There's a silence that makes me want to run. He steps up; it wobbles a bit. I catch his arms before he falls. I'm Godzilla and he's the little blonde lady I hold aloft. His face blushes emasculated pink. He looks smaller than ever up there. My crotch tingles with sadness. We smile and look the other way.

My nose now at *his* chin, we can start the scene. I keep my eyes fixed on his throat. I try and recall my lips on my hand, the soft, circular motions of my tongue. When the director shouts action, I freeze. I'm fixated on this man's Adam's apple. I wish it was a real apple, my stomach suddenly feels the emptiest it's ever been. My 'boyfriend' takes the initiative. He bends down from his hero podium, takes my chin in his hand and puts his lips on mine. My eyes squeeze together. His lips are soft and I think he's had as many chewing gums as I have. The overwhelming smell of peppermint oil makes my eyes water. It's not like the little kiss I've had before this which was a lip graze during a slow dance at the primary-school leavers disco. Everyone kissed and ran that night. I remember one girl kissed a boy in our class so fast and so hard, she knocked him to the ground and he broke his arm. She was long gone before anyone knew what had happened. This isn't kids' stuff. This is a real kiss. His tongue is touching my cheek. I'm telling mine to relax, but it's retreated to the back of my mouth like a scared gerbil. His head is moving and I'm aware mine is in a brace-like position. This must be like giving mouth-to-mouth to someone who's got whiplash. As we're suspended here, small details become disconcertingly big. I can hear tiny birds as loudly as fire alarms. I can feel the blood throbbing inside my ears, like I'm getting them pierced again. My crotch is like a hive of bees. My head slowly starts to move side to side like a metronome and I hear it tick every time it does.

When the director yells cut – 'my boyfriend' nearly falls off the box. He steadies himself on my shoulders as I use both hands to check if my lips are still there. He steps down and I cast a shadow over him. Is that it?

'I like your coat,' he says.

I don't remind him that it doesn't belong to me. We wipe our mouths with the backs of our hands and pretend to look for shooting stars in the daytime sky. I'm not disappointed when the director says we don't have to do it again.

Back at the trailers, we have a painfully thin hug goodbye. We barely touch each other. Then, he asks for my number. I don't particularly want to give it to him, but it feels like we're sort of – close now. I write it down for him. He folds it up and we wave goodbye. Why did he ask? Did he feel like he had to? Why did I say yes? I felt like I had to. He says he'll call me tomorrow.

The next day I wait by my phone. He might want to meet and kiss again. I want him to feel how much I've improved since the first time. I bring my hand up to my lips and start to practise again. Slowly, I try and put my whole fist inside my mouth. When my auntie calls from abroad I nearly punch all my teeth out. When she blocks the line speaking to my mum, I scream into my pillow for five minutes straight. The phone doesn't ring after that. I fall asleep in my clothes.

INT. ACTRESS'S BEDROOM. DAY.

ACTRESS *lies on her bed, her eyes open. She wears a mismatched bikini top and bottoms, a pair of goggles pulled up on her forehead. A bag with a half-stuffed swim towel just visible by the door.*

Her phone rings. 'Homegirl' flashes up on the screen.

ACTRESS *pauses. She takes the goggles off, tidies her hair back behind her ears, deep breath. She answers.*

> ACTRESS
>
> Oh, hi!

> HOMEGIRL
>
> Where the hell are you? Are you here? Are you away? Are you working? Are you in love? What's going on? No one's heard from you! I've left you a trillion messages! I started to do accents just to keep it entertaining. My life is going to shit obviously, that's not news, but I'm in hell and you've been DOA!

                    ACTRESS
I'm so sorry, hon. I'm away. I've
been away, working.

                    HOMEGIRL
Where? There wasn't an international
tone when I called?

ACTRESS *looks up at one of her obscure
film posters.* Un Chien Andalou.

                    ACTRESS
I'm in France. It's not that
international, really.

                    HOMEGIRL
Fuck, I'm jealous. I need to get out
of town.

                    ACTRESS
It's all really exciting.

                    HOMEGIRL
What is it?

                    ACTRESS
Hmm? Oh, babe, I'm just being called
away, speak later?

                    HOMEGIRL
Fuck that, you're not fucking hanging
up on me, it's taken a fucking age to
get you in person.

                    ACTRESS
It's long hours on this one.

                    HOMEGIRL
I'm pregnant.

Pause.

                    HOMEGIRL
Hello?

ACTRESS *covers the mouthpiece. Talks to
imaginary assistant.*

                    ACTRESS
Can I have five minutes? Thanks.

ACTRESS *takes her hand off the mouthpiece.*

                    HOMEGIRL
You there?

                    ACTRESS
Yeah.

                    HOMEGIRL
It's not ideal, so you don't need to
tell me that. I haven't told anyone,
not even him.

                    ACTRESS
And — are you sure?

                    HOMEGIRL
I'm putting the staff at the mini
Boots on the high street through
university right now. I've cleaned
them out of tests, which aren't
cheap. I think I've run out of piss
altogether. And they, all of them,
show up with the result — yeah,
your life is over.

                    ACTRESS
That's —

Her voice cracks.

                    ACTRESS
That's —

Tears start.

                    HOMEGIRL
    Are you — *crying*?

                     ACTRESS
    Your life isn't — it isn't —

She is choked.

                     ACTRESS
    Your *life* is just starting.
    There's life *inside* you.

                    HOMEGIRL
    Hello, I would like to know who you
    are and how much ransom you would
    like for my best friend's safe
    return.

Tears suddenly stream.

                     ACTRESS
                   (*sobbing*)
    Sorry. I'm just - so — happy —
    for — you.

                    HOMEGIRL
    What's wrong?

                    ACTRESS
    Nothing! This is just such a
    happy day.

                    HOMEGIRL
    Did you hear me?
    This signifies my slow descent.

ACTRESS *lets out a big cry.*

                    HOMEGIRL
    What's going on? You hate kids!
    That's why I wanted to talk to
    you first.

                    ACTRESS
    I love children.

                    HOMEGIRL
    You've always said children's
    laughter was like a fucking hot knife
    through butter.

                    ACTRESS
    Stop! OK, stop. People change.

ACTRESS *brings her knees up to her chin.*
The tears pump.

                    HOMEGIRL
It's me who's got the womb issue!
Not you!

                    ACTRESS
You're — my — best — friend -

                    HOMEGIRL
Yeah, now I feel like I have to ask
you if *you're* all right.

                    ACTRESS
I'm fine. It was just a surprise.
Sorry.

                    HOMEGIRL
Are you OK?

                    ACTRESS
                  (*sniffing*)
I'm fine, I'm fine.

Pause.

                    HOMEGIRL
Anyway, you probably have to go.

ACTRESS

No, no, I don't. This is important.
We've known each other since *we* were
babies. I'm coming to see you.

HOMEGIRL

From France?

ACTRESS

What? Oh! Yes, I'm coming right
away.

HOMEGIRL

OK ... Thanks. I've really needed —
that. I can't have you doing this
though, setting me off.

ACTRESS

I'm present and correct.

HOMEGIRL

Love you.

ACTRESS

Love you too.

HOMEGIRL

This is nuts ...

ACTRESS *gets up, with purpose. She walks
to the door. Stops. Turns. She opens her
jewellery box and puts the phone inside,
closes the lid.*

ACTRESS *lies down again, foetal
position. The ballerina on top of the
box spins to discordant music.*

                    HOMEGIRL
        Hello? Hello?

                              CUT TO:

Character: Trish, 16 yrs.
Breakdown: Teen mum with a contract and
a body to kill.
Project: Award-winning detective drama.
Notes from casting: Stunts required.

My current thoughts about pregnancy are very much in the 'how to prevent at all costs' category.

Any thoughts about motherhood stop at birth control.

Anything beyond that is nightmare.

I think I can act a mum though. I've been told I have a maternal energy.

My 'casting bracket' is shifting. Suddenly I'm too old for the parts I'm used to – tearaway daughter, street urchin, babysitter with a drug habit. But still too young for trainee policewoman and supply teacher with attitude. Looks like teen mums bridge the gap. A teen mum caught in the vicious world of underground arms dealing, that is. I bump people off to pay the rent and keep my child fed. I can get my head around the trained assassin part no problem. But I don't see how I'm going to be believable as a mum.

I make gun fingers in the mirror – looks cool. I make a cradle with my arms and it's just – no. I shake them out by my sides to get rid of the feeling. Murderer yes, mother not so much.

*

A very mature sixteen and a half – is what the producers say after my first audition. I could tell they loved me. They stared at me like a rare bird. I suppose it's hard to find a kid who can do this right.

'We'll call your agent.'

My hands are trembling when I leave the room.

I can't remember a single thing I did in there.

It's a blur of maternal and killer instincts.

Walking to the bus stop, strangers pass me and I feel dangerous, a killer walking among them. I put my hands in my pockets, sink my head down low in my collar, elbows out to the side as weapons. Don't be fooled by the baby face. I get into character. A police siren blares and I don't even flinch. I pull my stomach in under my T-shirt until it feels like a hollow egg, suck it all the way back to my ribs, to feel where the baby might have been. I point my gun fingers at a can in the gutter and fire – it jumps in the air, taken up on the speed of the traffic. Did I do that?

One baby is actually two – they cast a set of identical twins that they can rotate on shifts for the shoot, depending on their moods. The likeness to me is breathtaking. Casting the supporting members of black or dual-heritage families can make or break the believability of a fictional family in an instant. TV casting almost always drops the ball. Supporting artists lazily plucked by assistants from enormous directories without any thought given to the detail of their diasporic heritage or that of the family they're plonked into. If you're not looking for it, you don't see it, but there's a one-size-fits-all attitude applied too much on our small screens that leaves a great portion of the audience reaching for their remotes, angry as hell. But today, with my two girls, the detail is so spot on it's scary. They could be mine. I baby-talk with them, try and reassure their real mum. She's seen me wielding a gun for the most of the day. I tell her about sixth form and exams, my new – first – boyfriend. I'm a good kid. I'll be kind to her babies. Our babies.

At the top of a London tower block, we wait for dusk. Climactic scenes like the ones we're about to shoot always work best with a dramatic sunset. It's the police raid to end all police raids. I've left the getaway motorbike and the murder weapon dumped somewhere stupid, got lazy. A helmet with my DNA is what tips off the detective team. They have my flat surrounded with snipers. When they kick down the door, I'm supposed to start screaming. The director's told me to improvise so that there's believable overlapping while the cops read me my rights. As we wait for the light to be right, me and the babies bond. Twin number one is quick to laugh; we cuddle as fake blood is dabbed onto my head, a wound from the getaway chase. She's all wobbly and her little legs kick when I lift her. I jiggle her on my knee and she laughs, searches my face for more surprises. I blow a raspberry and it's hysterics all over again.

I'm suddenly very aware that, in a moment, I'm going to have to pick up a gun.

I can't imagine holding the two right now. I could before. I block it out until the last moment. I've already shot a man in cold blood today, it'll be fine.

The director shouts action and something doesn't feel right. I hold little laughing baby tight, the detectives cock their weapons on the other side of the door. I squeeze baby and squeeze my gun. I keep my knee bouncing to keep her happy and as my finger wraps round the trigger, I hope for the best.

It's taken ages to make her laugh, make her feel safe.

I keep my leg bouncing.

The cops kick the door in and it's a shattering sound.

I raise my gun, improvise, like I've been told.

'Kill my baby! You kill my baby then! Kill my baby! Kill me, you kill my baby!'

I'm shaking. I'm concentrating so hard on thinking what to say, I haven't tuned my ear to the baby screaming along with me. Her wailing is deafening – I have to shout louder to drown her out, which makes it worse. Her uncontrollable sobs are breaking my heart. She's pressed her mouth right up to my ear and curled her fingers round my cheek and hair, holding on for dear life. I can feel how hot she is, how her body shakes when her breath runs out. I can feel her tears in my ear. She's pressing herself into me, holding on to me like her mummy.

I'm shaking so much when they call cut, I feel my hands lose their grip. Real mum comes in like a bullet –

she's helped through a fake wall that splits the room in two.

My ears are ringing. The other twin is sobbing too, she sounds identical to her sister. We can all hear it now. The whole flat vibrates with baby fear.

'Can you make sure that the mum knows I didn't mean to do that? You told me to improvise.'

The director nods his head. He's got a priority and that's the light outside. We need to roll again and we're losing it.

'I didn't know what was going to happen, what was going to come out.'

'Don't worry, it's so believable, it's great. Let's go again, sound team need another one.'

People offer me water, a few minutes to compose myself, but I just want to go again straight away, get this over with. The second twin seems to have calmed down a bit, they swap the babies and I take my seat on the bed. This twin is all wriggles. She doesn't trust me at all. Her powerful fingers with surprisingly sharp nails jab my eyes and cheeks, she pulls my hair. I can't help but feel she's getting her own back for her sister.

My free arm attaches itself to the 9mm again. The cops burst in. I bring my gun up to meet them and twin two goes wild. I can't hear a thing. Then I notice that, to my real horror, the baby is looking at the gun. Her sister put her face into my neck, this twin is looking up and out at the weapon above her head.

I don't think there's anything about my eyes that says 'steely killer'. My face, which hasn't been able to lie since *I* was a baby, is definitely telling the story of how alarming all this is. They call cut. The lead actress is clearly upset. I see her whisper something to the producer. He comes over and tells me that they won't do another take because they're losing the light out of the window. Yeah, right. Your lead actress just told you she'll walk if you keep ruining these little girls' childhoods.

I grit my teeth, aimlessly turn the sawn-off shotgun in my hand.

The babies let out hypersonic cries in Real Mum's ears. She bounces them, shakes her head. She probably had her fingers crossed for a Pampers commercial.

The director and his assistant rub their foreheads. They have a new verdict. We *do* need to go one more time. There's more rubbing of heads and throwing up of arms; the leading actress who complained gets out her phone and calls her agent in the corner.

'Let's try baby number one please.'

Real Mum looks like she might collapse. I have to prise first twin's fingers off her mother's arm. It's a war I don't want to win. As soon as she's free, she buries her hot face in my cheek again, clings to me. I'm the nearest thing to a mum she's got as the fake wall goes up again.

'Can we do this, *please*?'

My voice sounds grown up.

They call action quickly, the light is almost gone. I bounce baby, get my finger round the trigger and when the cops burst in I give them hell. I *really* want them out this time, I *need* them to leave me and baby alone. I don't know what I scream this time, but the pit of my stomach is a ball of fire. I'm a lioness with a cub. The police have no choice but to back out of the door, their hands up.

When they call cut I know it's over. We won't have to do that again, the scene can't get realer than that. A few people clap. I look away. Real Mum jumps past the fake wall and scoops up baby on the hip. She's already got her coat and bag together.

The babies are whisked off set before I even get to give them a proper squeeze. Let them know I'm not really a bad person. I try to follow Real Mum down the hall, but they want to do a close-up of me and the gun and I get called back to set. The camera is just on my face, I'll raise the gun and do all the action and the screaming but they'll frame the baby out this time. Couldn't we have just done that in the first place?

It's eerily silent in there without my babies.

I feel like a hollow egg.

'So amazing, so so amazing. How did you do that?' coos the director at the end.

Back in my dressing room I lift my T-shirt up, scoop my stomach in against my ribs. Turn to the side, do it again, and again. More, until it hurts.

INT. CASTING STUDIO, WEST LONDON. DAY.

ACTRESS *sits uncomfortably on a stool
in front of a photographer's spool of
paper. The early-evening sunlight falls
on her face. She closes her eyes as the
natural light is replaced by bright,
synthetic film lights.*

ASSISTANT *works the camera.*

DIRECTOR *sits in a jacket and hat, arms
folded behind a monitor, ACTRESS's face
in close-up right in front of him.*

                    DIRECTOR
     We're excited.

                    ACTRESS
     Me too.

                    DIRECTOR
     You look a little tired today.

ACTRESS *opens her eyes.*

                    ACTRESS
     Sorry?

DIRECTOR

You look a little tired. You want to
freshen your make-up while we wait?

Silence.

ACTRESS *stands to get her bag. Her top*
rides up, her navel shows in close-up on
the screen.

DIRECTOR

Clothes are way better this time.

She pulls it back down.

She applies some peach fluid underneath
her eyes, the bottle is nearly empty.
She presses it into her dark sockets
with her finger. DIRECTOR watches her
do it on the screen.

DIRECTOR

Something, here — (*He gestures.*)
For the shine.

ACTRESS *takes an old powder puff out from*
her bag, pads at her forehead, her nose,
her chin.

                    DIRECTOR
Now you look a little dead, all one
colour.

ACTRESS *rummages, takes a coloured gloss
out of the floral pouch. She pulls out the
small wand inside and moves it slowly
over her lips.* DIRECTOR *watches up close
as they gleam, like they're wet.*

                    ACTRESS
My mum bought me this. Good timing.

                    DIRECTOR
That's better. OK, we're going to roll.

                    ACTRESS
What scenes should I do?

                    DIRECTOR
No scenes today. Not until Mikey
gets here.

                    ACTRESS
Who's Mikey?

                    DIRECTOR
Mikey is who you're testing with
today.

                    ACTRESS
What does that actually mean?

                    DIRECTOR
For chemistry. We want him for the
part of Alan, the aerospace engineer
turned lover for you, of course. The
producers need to see you click. OK,
we're rolling — turn your head to
the side?

ACTRESS *turns her head to the left.*
Pause.

                    ACTRESS
The science in the script is quite
interesting.

                    DIRECTOR
Other side.

ACTRESS *turns her head.*

                    ACTRESS
Vaccines of the future — who'll have
access to them?

                    DIRECTOR
And back to me.

ACTRESS *turns back to the camera.*

> DIRECTOR
> Good to know your angles too.
> (*To* ASSISTANT.)
> Can you make a note not to shoot her
> from the right? A note about under
> here (*he gestures around his eye
> sockets*) that will have to be for
> the VFX team to deal with.

ACTRESS *looks down, pretends not to hear.*

> ACTRESS
> If only Dr Kollins's science was
> real. The world would be in a lot
> less trouble.

> DIRECTOR
> OK, now move back.

ACTRESS *moves the stool backwards.*
ASSISTANT *moves the light.*
As she stands, her top rides up again.
She pulls it down, self-conscious.

> DIRECTOR
> Let your top go, it's fine. Don't let
> anyone shoot you from another side.

Left is where you work best, with
most lenses.

The camera zooms in on ACTRESS*'s face.*

A knock at the door. MIKEY, *30s,
ruggedly handsome, a new talent, bounds
into the room.*

                    MIKEY
      Hey!

                    DIRECTOR
      Mikey! Great, you made it. Great
      jacket.

                    MIKEY
      Thanks. Sorry I'm late.

                    DIRECTOR
      You're a busy man!

                    ACTRESS
      Hey.

                    MIKEY
      Hey.

ACTRESS *and* MIKEY *shake hands.*

                    DIRECTOR
    Oh yes, sorry, you haven't met. You
    OK to dive straight in?

                    ACTRESS
    Uh, yeah.

                    MIKEY
    Yep.

    ASSISTANT *takes MIKEY's jacket, adjusts
    his hair.*

                    DIRECTOR
    That looks great, Mikey.

    *The camera zooms in. MIKEY's face is
    big on the screen. He moves his head in
    a fluid left/right motion without being
    prompted. ACTRESS stares.*

                    DIRECTOR
    Thank you, Mikey.

                    MIKEY
    Yep, sure. Shall we get on with the
    scene?

                         DIRECTOR
            Absolutely, you good?

He nods at ACTRESS.

                          ACTRESS
            Which scenes?

                         DIRECTOR
            If you swap, so she can be on her
            best side?

*They swap chairs. ASSISTANT brings some
pages of script over.*

                         ASSISTANT
            Here you go.

                           MIKEY
            Shall we start on thirty-four?

                         DIRECTOR
            Yeah, thirty-four, great idea, Mikey.

*They start to read from the pages.
DIRECTOR watches them both on the
screen.*

                    ACTRESS
        'What are you doing here? I thought
        you left the mission?'

                    MIKEY
        'I had to see you. Make sure you
        were safe.'

                    ACTRESS
        'You disappeared ...'

                    MIKEY
        'I've been here the whole time. See
        that hovercraft?'

MIKEY *points somewhere in the middle*
distance. ACTRESS *turns to look —*
without turning too far from her best
side.

                    ACTRESS
        'You were following me this whole
        time?'

                    MIKEY
        'I told you. I'd never leave you.
        Not on this godforsaken planet.'

                    ACTRESS
Sorry, that's my line? 'Godforsaken
planet'?

                    DIRECTOR
Cut.

                    MIKEY
I thought I'd try something, seemed
like something he would say.

                    DIRECTOR
Worked great. Next scene.

MIKEY *leans in to kiss* ACTRESS. ACTRESS
*looks out towards the camera, looks down
the barrel, her confused stare blown up
big on the TV screen.*

                    ACTRESS
Are we —?

                    DIRECTOR
Top of the next scene. Don't break it ...

MIKEY *takes her face in his hands.*
ACTRESS *looks stiff. He kisses her.
It intensifies.* ACTRESS *pulls away.*

                    ACTRESS
'Thank you for always being there.
No one told me how lonely saving the
planet would be.'

                    DIRECTOR
Cut, great, this is so great.

                    ACTRESS
I wasn't really ready for -

                    DIRECTOR
You two have great chemistry!

                    ACTRESS
What happened to all the science?

                    DIRECTOR
We're still playing with that.

                    MIKEY
That was really good for me.

                    DIRECTOR
Me too.

                    ACTRESS
I think if we'd said we were going to
do the kiss, I would have — I thought —

                    DIRECTOR
You let the moment take you, it
worked. Yep. Why don't you both
take five and we'll do your close-ups,
Mikey, and set the room up for some
of the karate stuff, you still good to
show us some of that today?

                    MIKEY
For sure! Space karate!

                    DIRECTOR
You'll hear from us later.

MIKEY *and* ACTRESS *stand in the corridor.*
ACTRESS *puts her coat on.*

                    MIKEY
That was really cool. Thanks for
going with the kiss, I was trying
something. I won't be long, we
should have a drink.

                    ACTRESS
I don't know you.

                     MIKEY
Sure. But you *recognise* me?

                                    CUT TO:

Character: Charlotte, early 20s.
Breakdown: Disfigured recluse looking for love finds face-transplant donor and a husband. Lead.
Project: Romance/feature.
Notes from casting: Please submit ethnic actors only.

Graduate actors need photographs. Of their faces. Something potential agents can sell you on. To show your 'type'. Not as much *who you are* but who you *could* be.

It's how you will get work.

For the past three years, twenty-one of us have committed to a degree in 'acting'. It's the Cinderella's coach of qualifications. It may or may not turn into a giant pumpkin come graduation day.

Three years of training and, like an athlete, it's time to compete. You're to live like a professional from now on. Eat and sleep like a professional, your student pastimes should draw to a close. Takeaways should be replaced with vegetables and alcohol should no longer be neon in colour.

I choose the only female photographer recommended on the pre-grad noticeboard.

The day arrives and I pick out the T-shirts that are the most neutral in my collection. Basically the only ones without a band name or a deep home-made slash down the front. The key is to be beige, castable. The industry needs to project onto your face. I throw in a completely unsuitable shirt for good measure.

A tiny woman welcomes me into a large period house with intimidating views of the Mersey. Her thighs don't remotely touch. Her wrists look the same thickness as the laces on my shoe. How will she take the weight of a professional camera?

'When the industry decided the camera should be turned off me, I decided to turn it on other people!' she shouts over her shoulder, pouring freshly made coffee.

There are framed photos of her everywhere. On the walls, the piano, the windowsills.

'From my days as a *modela*.'

She uses a mock-Italian accent for maximum impact.

'First it was the pageants, then I never stopped. Never a supermodel, never tall enough. *You* could barely fit through the door! You have the height of a model! With your height? The world would have been mine!'

Paris, New York, Milan, they all came calling and some of the greats have shot her face, the way she's about to shoot mine. She learned from some of the biggest models around and it would never have slowed down if she hadn't had children.

'The industry is cruel, you might as well know it now. Just because you love it, doesn't mean it has to love you back.'

I look for photos of the children she talks about, but find none.

'Thankfully I'm an actor, not a model.'

She laughs.

'Same thing. You don't sell, you don't work.'

She says the coffee isn't just for coffee. It's so she can study me. How I move. She won't be happy unless she captures a piece of my soul.

'These are going to be intimate portraits so we have to be intimate.'

I don't drink coffee but try and sip as confidently as possible. She takes one of the framed photographs and brings it close to me.

'How old do you think I am here?'

Before I can guess she tells me she's nineteen. She asks me how old *I* am.

'Twenty.'

'And do you think you could fit into this outfit I'm wearing here?'

It doesn't look like I could. She laughs hysterically, like she's at a party.

She takes more photos off the wall, produces them from bookcases. I consistently fail to guess her age and dress size. Young people from bygone eras always tend to look older, so I struggle. It distresses her. She makes more coffee. I can't have any more, my chest is vibrating and I can feel the early cramps of diarrhoea. I don't know how this works. Do I make her aware of the time? I can feel the professional make-up I've bought on a budget flaking off. I ask for water.

'How much water do you drink a day?'

It's mostly cut-price beers and spirits at the moment.

'Four or five litres?'

It resounds as a lie. I read that in an interview with a famous actress. I'd have to have a catheter if I drank that much. She goes quiet as she passes me a bottle from the fridge.

'You should drink a lot more. You look dehydrated.'

'Yes. Thank you. I will.'

'Take it from me. Under your eyes? Water to start with, to hydrate, and then when you can afford the surgery –'

'I'm sorry?'

Water dribbles out of my mouth. I feel as though I've just been thrown out of a moving van into a dark pool of water.

'Surgery?'

'It's these –'

She makes a big deal of taking her glasses off and squinting at me.

'Age is cruel on the eyes!'

I sip cold coffee, just to give my hands something else to do, as she leans in, her breath is stale.

'These. *These.*'

She traces a line with her finger around her own eyes, close to where her glasses have made purplish indentations.

'These ridges. Under your eyes.'

Now she traces the skin around *my* eyes. Her finger smells like sour milk.

'It's a simple procedure to drain them, drain this fluid so they come down. Your eyes won't be so – *pronounced*. If you drink water they won't be as dark. You won't have the swelling. Like a boxer.'

'I've had deeply set eyes since birth, it's a family trait. I think.'

'Yes. Your whole face is circles. You see, the camera doesn't like circles at *all*. It likes squares, lines, angles. On camera your face will – stretch.'

She points at one of her old modelling clippings, the light bouncing off her angular face. She raises her eyebrows, encouraging me.

'I am a square.'

'Yes, yes, I see.'

I clasp my hands under the table.

'You? Are a circle.'

She stiffens her finger, brings it back towards my face. Slowly and deliberately, she traces *every* circle she finds.

My eyes. My mouth. Two circles on each cheek. My chin. My nose is a circle. I see little perforated lines appear in the air as she does it, the ones you might find on a sewing pattern. Or a patient before surgery. They swirl, in circles, every place she points her bony wand. The lines dance in front of my eyes. I think the caffeine is making me hallucinate. They slowly join together, forming the rough outline of a comic-strip character.

The character is a huge white circle and has my outsized face imprinted on it, like a cartoon moon. Animated letters swirl and pulse above my head, they're made up of the same perforated dashes, plastic-surgery markings. The letters bounce up and down and into each other, they start to merge and form a title – 'The Adventures of Circle Head'. The comic strip comes to life. *I* am Circle Head. My tiny stick legs buckle under the weight of my huge circle head as I walk down a square cobbled street in Square-topia. There's a square that vomits at the sight of me, a square mother hides the square eyes of her square children. A square policeman approaches, off balance on his square bicycle as he tries to blow his square whistle to break up the square crowd. A square man crashes his square car into a square coconut tree, square coconuts litter his car bonnet as square smoke spirals into the square clouds.

'Did you bring options for clothes?'

The pen marks dissolve.

'Um, yes.'

'Choose something light to start. I know exactly what we need to do with you, we need to be outside. You need natural light for your face to come alive!'

She has this Italian accent that comes and goes. I'm going to cry.

'Where's your bathroom?'

I go to the toilet and pull my top off. Two breasts – circles. Tops of shoulders – circles. Clavicle – circles. Armpits – circles. The caffeine has dried out my stomach to the shape of, yes, a circle. The tears that threaten to come have made a circle lump in my burning throat. I look at my stupid face and hear comical lift muzak.

Out on the street, the *modela*'s approach to posing doesn't seem to have contemporised. I find myself in an eighties ad campaign, striking dated poses such as crouching by a kerb leaning my chin on my hand, lounging against a brick wall with my thumbs in my belt buckle, looking coyly over my shoulder with one hand on my hip in front of a tree. She's snapping away and I just *can't* get into it. Circular Spirograph doodles keep dancing in front of the camera, distracting me. I can see my big distorted circle head upside down in the black of the lens. My face morphs into a cartoon again. This time Circle Head's adventures have taken her to a square zoo, she's trapped behind square bars, a square sign reads 'Do Not Feed'. Big circle tears drop into the dried grass in her square feed bowl.

'More power! Give it to me! You look distracted!'

Her wrists look so weak waving that huge camera in the air.

'Can I change my T-shirt?'

'Yeah! We need to shake this up a bit, darling!'

She uses the word 'darling' like there are other people listening.

I duck behind the tree and pull off my white T-shirt. I lean my ribs against the trunk for a bit. Let the bark pierce me.

'Come on! We don't want to lose the light, baby!'

She imitates the misogynist banter of the sixties legends who shot her.

'Like you mean it, come *on*, give it to me, there's something you're hiding, tell me a naughty secret with your eyes. Give it to me, give it to *me*!'

That Italian accent just comes and goes as it pleases, it's jarring. *Is* she Italian? Or is this all part of the Euro-centric smut-ographer impersonation? A model friend had told me about a legendary photographer going up behind women on shoots and putting his hands around their necks, pretending to strangle them if they don't deliver. He started slapping vaginas when he got really famous. He was a Goliath in the modelling world, an artist, everyone was afraid they'd never work again if they crossed him. If you became his muse, your agents would suggest you let him touch you inappropriately until your career sky-rocketed. The work would pay for the therapy. He pleasured himself in front of my friend and two other models in a lift. His gallery was too busy with a huge retrospective exhibited in his honour to follow up on the rumours.

The light fades, me and Circle Head boing along, bouncing off things all dumb and squidgy as *she* moves squarely with ease. I manage a smile, a laugh even, in front of her lens. I've washed pots for three months to pay for this. I can't let her ruin it. I need to go back with good photos. I have to show the industry how much they want me. How versatile my T-shirt collection and I are. One photo is worth a thousand words. I can't look like a balloon someone's let go of. I need to create the identity I want for myself. Maybe that's what's up with Austin Powers here. She *can't* use photos to define her any more. No one wants to project their dreams onto her now. It's just her. In the real world. With faded clippings where photos of her grandkids could sit.

It's nearly dark. We walk back to the house by the river.

We pass a giant digger pulled up by the side of the bank, silhouetted in the half-light. She jumps up and down, pops her lens cap like champagne, edges me up towards it with her painfully sharp elbow.

'Climb on the wheel! This is perfect! Let's be free! We have a little of the roll left, darling! This is spontaneous!'

I slip my favourite shirt over my head. If I'm going out, I'm going out as myself.

I scale the digger, its enormous jagged wheels triggering the most vivid hallucination yet.

Circle Head is lying in a square hospital bed, perforated lines all over her circle body. A square backstreet doctor takes his square syringe and plunges it into Circle Head's circle vein.

'Drape yourself on the wheel, it's divine!'

The square anaesthetic takes hold, and then the noise of a square chainsaw coming to life. Circle blood sprays on the square wall.

'Darling, this is the shot!'

When Circle Head comes to, her circular body aches. Spots of red all over the white square sheets. A kindly square nurse appears with square bandages and gasps a square gasp at the sight. Where she was round, she is now straight. Square stitches sprout from right angles that used to be curved. The healing wounds heave with square yellow pus. Circle Head stares at her new straight lines.

'It's better this way.'

I shut my eyes tight. When I open them, the *modela* is yelling.

'Why did you do that? You ruined the last shot!'

I jump down off the wheel.

INT. EXPENSIVE MALL, WEST LONDON. DAY.

ACTRESS *exits the revolving door.*
Expensive perfume hits her lungs as she
slopes through the cosmetics department.
She looks around, purposeful. 'She is
life' - says a pink neon sign for a
reliable brand. ACTRESS *heads that way.*

Testers sit in their plastic holes. ACTRESS
picks up a bottle, pumps beige liquid onto
her finger, rubs it into her jawline. It
glistens like wet chalk against her skin.

>   ACTRESS
>   This doesn't look like a suntan.

MAN IN THE MALL *stops applying lip gloss*
to himself.

>   MAN IN THE MALL
>   Can I help?

>   ACTRESS
>   It's called Suntan. This doesn't look
>   like a suntan. On my skin.

>   MAN IN THE MALL
>   Ooh. OK.

He glides closer. He selects another bottle, pumps more beige liquid onto his own hand, pats it onto ACTRESS's face.

                    MAN IN THE MALL
          No, you're not Sable.

He chooses another bottle, pumps, pats.

                    MAN IN THE MALL
          Not, Latte. Maybe a mixture of Sable
          and Latte.

                    ACTRESS
          In a way.

                    MAN IN THE MALL
          You're definitely not Suntan. Did you
          try Honeycomb?

                    ACTRESS
          No.

                    MAN IN THE MALL
          Here we go. If I apply it with a
          brush -

He pumps the pump, makes a big to-do of rolling a small brush in the liquid before applying it to ACTRESS*'s jawline on the other side.*

                    MAN IN THE MALL
          That's a much better match for you.

ACTRESS *turns her head to the mirror. Another glistening snail trail gleams in contrast to the deeper tone of the skin she's in. Her jawline is a mass of mismatched stripes.*

                        ACTRESS
          Do you have any other —?

                    MAN IN THE MALL
          Honeycomb is the darkest we go.

                        ACTRESS
          Nothing after Honeycomb? It seems to
          be lighter than Suntan — even.

                    MAN IN THE MALL
          If you think about it, a suntan is
          actually just a version of actual
          skin, whereas honey is a food.

                        ACTRESS
          What?

                    MAN IN THE MALL
          Let's try Honeycomb and Latte mixed.

He does the same dance of the pumps and
swirls the centre of ACTRESS*'s forehead.*
It's a pinky-grey circle. ACTRESS *takes*
in the stripes on her jaw and now the
orb on her head.

                       ACTRESS
          I look like I'm in a cult.

                    MAN IN THE MALL
          These are the colours we carry.
          I think there's a new range due
          though.

                       ACTRESS
          This brand is nearly a century old.

                    MAN IN THE MALL
          It can take a century to work it out,
          exactly.

ACTRESS *smiles. She pumps all the pumps*
on her hand and blends them with her
finger.

                    ACTRESS
They're all the same colour.
Porcelain, Sable, Suntan, Honeycomb.
Latte is white.

                MAN IN THE MALL
He coughs. Excuse me. There's a
Gingerbread due out in the autumn. Do
you want a wet wipe?

                    ACTRESS
No. I'm going to leave them there
for a while. If anyone asks what
brand they are, I'm going to say
yours.

                MAN IN THE MALL
Might I take you through our new lip
shades?

                    ACTRESS
I haven't left the house in a while.

                MAN IN THE MALL
As I say, there's a Gingerbread due
in the autumn.

                    ACTRESS

I needed make-up to stop looking tired.
So, what colour would you say my skin
is? Looking at it now. Look at me.
What colour do you see?

                  MAN IN THE MALL

I ... um ...
Mocha-chocalata-yaya?

                    ACTRESS

Did you just quote a Patti LaBelle
song?

                              CUT TO:

Character: TBC, 21.
Breakdown: The only woman in the film.
Project: Feature-length special/UK
broadcast/TV.
Notes from casting: All male parts cast,
waiting for the right actress to fill
this role. As the only woman in the film,
this is a great opportunity for any
actress to shine among a stellar cast.

I bumped into him the other day. In a cinema. The irony.
He hugged me. It was a casual encounter. There were
people around.

'When was the last time I saw you?' he said.

He told me I looked well.

I felt the chunks rise in my throat.

I *could* remember the last time I saw him.

I knew he remembered too because when he saw
me, standing in the queue, when our eyes met – his eyes
flickered. His whole brain flickered. And I could see. I
could see he hadn't thought about that night again, until that moment. Whereas I'd had to search for months
for a place to put it.

I acted polite. *We* acted polite until –

'You shouldn't have hugged me like that.'

This is what happens when I tell myself not to say
something.

For a moment he looked scared. Real fear. I didn't drop my gaze, not this time. He smiled, waved to some friends behind me and was gone.

I ran home, missed the film I was queuing for – I didn't want to be in a dark room with him.

When I play it back in my head, it sounds like the opening dialogue from an eighties porn film. He tells me he is an executive producer on a film that has just lost its lead actress. He needs a replacement, someone with star quality. For the right girl, this could be a huge break.

I've just come offstage. The West End bar is too loud. He says we should take a walk. Out in the street we talk about film, art and money. How one kills the other. He calls me a real artist and, for whatever reason, I feel high. He says he could tell that I loved film. How dare he talk to me about love. He knew what he was doing when he separated me from my friends. Knows I'll be open. Just offstage and open as anything. Knows that if he waits long enough, talking about real art, that the adrenaline and his bottle of champagne will kick in. He keeps saying the word 'gravitas', that he needs someone with great looks, but gravitas.

This part is to be a 'woman for all women', he says, as he walks me further and further away from anyone I know. He wants to start improvising scenes, straight away, says he just has such a good feeling about me being *the one*.

As we walk, messages start to ping on my phone. 'Where are you? Did I see you leave with someone?' I switch it to silent. We'll head back once I've managed to secure an audition. A block from the theatre, he stops me underneath a street light. He wants to look in my eyes. See the strength that this character would need, see it in me. There it is. Perfect for the opening scene. He wants to measure himself against me, check how tall I am, marches me over to a brick wall. No point in going any further if I'm going to tower over the leading man. He slides his hand over my head, measuring me up against the graffiti. Perfect. Just the right size. He'll let the American producers know. Then he pushes the top of my head down. Says I make him feel small. We laugh.

It's all coming together. He wants to start rehearsing, prep me so that I'll wow the other execs.

He sets the scene, straight out of the script. The amazing, strong, complex heroine – me – is trying to fight off her abusive boyfriend. He comes home drunk again and it's make or break for their relationship.

'This is the scene where she wins our hearts and then breaks them.'

If he is going to cast me over a Hollywood actress, I'll have to really show him what I've got.

'What does he do to her?' I ask.

'Just react,' he says, smiling. 'Play, come on.'

'I don't know, I've got a show tomorrow.' That's me starting to smell the stink bomb.

'She's a *survivor*. A desert flower. You're perfect for this.'

Bad lies on bad breath. He starts teasing, pinching me, on my waist. Telling me to loosen up.

The best actors are relaxed actors.

He calls action and, among the trees and the dark, I play along. I play along, because I've always played along. It's what I do.

I want this part. Have always wanted a part like this. I identify with the desert flowers of this world.

He leans into me and his eyes shift.

He is trying to knock me over.

I push him back. He falls, limp and drunk.

'Oh my God, are you OK?

'I'm in character!' he whispers. I laugh at myself.

He comes at me again, the abusive boyfriend lines slurring out of his mouth.

I improvise as best I can, pushing as hard as I can.

My arms are shaking. I'm not fit. I need a break. He takes both my ears in his hands, gently, and then screams in my face. Holds me eye to eye in a headlock.

'Why do you hurt me over and over?'

I lose my lines, with spit in my eyes and over my lips. He pulls me towards him. 'Hold me.'

'I'm tired of the excuses!'

That's quite a good line actually.

I shout it over and over until it hurts my chest. His grip loosens and I can breathe. I push him again.

'Harder.'

I push him again.

'Harder.'

Again, in his ribs.

Then he catapults into me, throws his arms round my neck and squeezes, tells me he loves me and doesn't want to hurt me. Grabs my face. I'm panting, hard. He is a big man. He moves his lips to the side of my mouth. I feel his drool and freeze. Too real. I duck my head and pretend to cry. A tragic heroine on the verge. I direct myself in my head – the objective of the scene is how to get out of it. As long as I'm in character, I'm safe.

I let him grab my waist, move his hands lazily to the top of my hips, touch everything, move himself against me like a worm.

'Let this happen.'

He teases his tongue out. My mouth is as cold as the sea. The smell of stale saliva under my nose.

He stares at me all dopey afterwards. Like he just had the best kiss of his life and like I feel the same. All I'm thinking about is him being diagnosed with something incurable. It's the best acting I've ever done.

'I don't want to do this any more.'

Then silence.

That silence.

His eyes glaze over like a shark before an attack.

There's a change that happens in the air, like being in a lift to the basement.

I don't know what I'm waiting for, what's coming. What he's weighing up. I go to a quiet place, the quietest, strongest place inside myself, where anything could happen and I would survive.

Suddenly, a jolt in his whole body, like coming to after a long sleep. I shield my face.

He laughs.

'I had no idea you were *that* good!'

He slaps my arms.

He does not ask for my professional details.

'You've got a special talent.'

He runs for a passing taxi.

I'm not sure how long I stand in that dark square listening to the air.

I get a cab too. I can't afford it, but I even tip the driver. It makes me feel powerful. When he asks what I do, I tell the driver I'm an actress living in Hollywood, back in the city for a break. At home, I double-lock the door and sleep with the lamp on. It could have been so much worse, I tell myself. I've got friends who've survived far, far worse. This was a nasty bite, not being eaten alive. There *is* a difference.

Months later, a man with the same aftershave passes me in the street and I cower in a doorway. People ask if I'm OK.

INT. ACTRESS'S BATHROOM. DAY.

ACTRESS *pulls her pyjama top up,*
checks her breasts for lumps. She
turns to the side, sucks her stomach
in to the extreme. Ribs emerge. It
looks painful. She lets the air go and
watches her stomach bloat outwards.
She stops to scrub her hands through
her hair, like washing it. It's an
aggressive act. She lets her hair fall
over her face in a tangled mess. She
leaves it for a moment. Slowly, she
lifts her hand underneath the matted
mess, revealing her eyes. They have
tears in them.

ACTRESS*'s phone starts ringing from the*
dirty clothes basket where it's been
tossed. She shakes some dirty knickers
off the screen. 'Agent' flashes up again
and again.

ACTRESS *wipes her eyes and pulls her top*
down. She pauses before answering.

                    ACTRESS
        Heeeeeeey!

                    AGENT
      Hey, glad I caught you. Is it a good
      time?

                    ACTRESS
      Great time, good, dandy time.

                    AGENT
      You in the bathroom?

                    ACTRESS
      What?

                    AGENT
      There's an echo? Are you in a
      bathroom?

                    ACTRESS
      No, that's the -

ACTRESS *looks around the room. Her eyes*
fall on a miniature trawler in a bottle.
A trinket from a seaside trip long ago.
Gathering dust.

                    ACTRESS
      I'm ... on a boat.

                    AGENT
Wow!

                    ACTRESS
Yeah, my friend has a boat, we had —
a party — on it — last night. I'm
still here.

                    AGENT
Glam! Well, you'll be on many more
boats soon!

                    ACTRESS
Oh?

                    AGENT
When we find you that life-changing
role. They've gone a different way on
the sci-fi.

                    ACTRESS
Oh. I thought the screen test —

                    AGENT
The producers didn't think you and
Mikey had quite enough chemistry.

                    ACTRESS
So, they cast Mikey?

                    125

                    AGENT
Yep.

                    ACTRESS
But not me.

                    AGENT
It's not personal. His latest movie
is making a lot of money at the box
office.

                    ACTRESS
Right.

                    AGENT
For what it was made for, it's a
smash.

                    ACTRESS
His *stock* is *up*.

                    AGENT
As is yours! In a different way.

                    ACTRESS
Is this because I didn't show my
physique?

ACTRESS *stares ahead at the mirror. She rolls her hips sexily, bites her lip.*

> AGENT
>
> No! It's one of those things. They said you did a great job. Though, they did mention you looked a bit tired, maybe that your hair is a little short, a little on the edgy side for them — probably. Not to worry.

> ACTRESS
>
> Living in space is quite edgy.

> AGENT
>
> Absolutely! But anyway, other than that there's so much more to explore. There's a superhero franchise that they're switching male to female, very cool. You do mixed martial arts, right?

ACTRESS *stares straight ahead, starts running the cold tap.*

> ACTRESS
>
> Sorry, we're pulling in to dock, I should go.

The water splashes up her chest, her arms.

                                        CUT TO:

```
Character: TBC, mid-20s.
Breakdown: Savvy sex worker with a
conscience. Supporting role.
Notes from casting: Nudity/sex/simulated
sex acts required. No script available.
```

On Gumtree, there are loads of jobs for restaurant
hostesses. I don't think I've ever heard of a restaurant hostess before but they're in demand. I used to
be on the door on club nights. I'm inscrutable. I'm
not, I let everyone in, but always the right people. I
somehow always know just the right latecomers to
add to the guest list. I've got a good radar and the
nights end up the better for it. I think I'd be great at
seating people in a restaurant, especially classy ones.
I think I could get scarily good at snobbishly turning
people away too. I can do this. Some of the ads say
they provide 'costume'. I don't even have to worry
about buying a new outfit! I've got this. Anything is
better than what the jobcentre wanted to send me up
for – an *elf* – for Santa's grotto in the local mall. I'm
five foot ten! What kind of elves do they think Santa's
breeding? I get a reply from one place really quickly
and some quiet alarm bells start to ring. Firstly, it's
not in the good part of town that they claimed it was.
It's not Knightsbridge, it's nearer Heathrow. And it's
not strictly a restaurant, it's a karaoke bar that does
food. Apparently a hit with businessmen in transit.

OK ... Not *exactly* the image I was going for ... I ask what I might be asked to do if my duties don't include reservations and seating people. I get a couple of lines in reply.

> You would be entertaining and hosting the
> businessmen. Do you have your own bikini?

I jump away from the computer. Needless to say the other responses come back with similar requirements. I can't touch my keyboard for a while. It feels like it's dripping in slime. I didn't ask for that. Why can't restaurant hostess just mean restaurant hostess?

A few weeks later, life imitates art. I land a much-needed job. A High-Class Escort in an improvised script. I take it that it's assumed I would know what a high-class escort might do and say, as there's no support in that department. I go to my computer and start again. I type 'high-class escorts' into Google. Wow. There's a billion. I scroll through and through and through and through. Decadence, Diamond, Elite. There's a lot of crossover with high-class taxi firms here. I click on one. I don't know what denotes 'high class', I've never done this before. Each female escort appears by name in alphabetical order. There are studio photos of the women, and what look like girls, in their underwear. Their names appear highlighted to make it easy to click straight to their profiles.

There's a girl of the month. I click on her. She's got one of the more real photos on her profile to balance out the studio glamour. She's taken it in a mirror at home, it's full length, she's topless, wearing a neon orange thong. She looks like a girl I went to school with. As well as the photo she has some reviews, which are hidden, you have to pay to read those. OK. There's her name, nationality, her height, her measurements, hair and eye colour, a note to say whether she's available for international travel and a list of acronyms. What do these mean? I get closer to the screen, a pop-up for a porn site leaps up, it's flashing purple in my face, 'girls begging for anal', a woman on all fours spreading her cheeks. I click off, click off, click *off*. I feel bad. I don't want that woman to beg for anal. Why is my heart racing? I feel responsible. I feel like it's me spreading that woman's arse cheeks, with my own hands. This world. I negotiate my way back to find the agency contact details. I flinch every time the page refreshes itself. New tabs flash in the distance: 'HOT GIRLS WANT YOU – NOW!' I pick up my phone and dial. It rings. I didn't expect it to actually ring. I grab a pen and a scrap of paper. The woman who picks up is instantly reassuring. Her tone is cheerful and matter-of-fact. It's like I'm ordering flat-pack furniture. I tell her I'm nervous. She tells me not to be. I think she thinks I'm calling for myself, to become an escort myself. I tell her that I'm not. I'm not calling to become an escort, but I sort of feel like I am.

'I just want to know what's involved.'

'Aw, bless ya.'

My voice is wobbling and cracking all over the place, my palms are sweating.

'I'm so nervous, I'm sorry.'

'Don't be silly. I'll take you through it, you wouldn't have to do it all if you join, you could tell me what feels right.'

The woman is so lovely, we click. I feel safe with her. She's kind, motherly.

'You've got a lovely voice, you could just do the phones if you wanted.'

'I just wondered what all the letters were, on the website. What they mean?'

'Aw, bless you. OK, so you would have seen A or A-level? That's anal. OK?'

BBBJ is bare back and blow job.

'OK?'

CIM is come in mouth.

'OK?'

DFK is deep French kissing.

'Because you know, some of the girls don't like to do anal – to *kiss*, I mean! Haha! Sorry, I got my words wrong, sorry, some won't do *kissing*. I'm a bit tired today.'

Not all the girls do anal but most do.

'Then there's GFE.'

The Girlfriend Experience.

'Those men often won't want sex.'

What they pay for is the experience of having a girlfriend. You go on dates, sleep over, drive him to the airport.

'How about I give you the code and you can get into the reviews section of our website and take a look?'

She reads out the code and I scribble it down – my palms wet.

'OK? Have a look and you can call me back any time, OK? You don't have to be nervous.'

She's so lovely. She's so lovely, I could consider it. The Girlfriend Experience ... Just play someone's girlfriend for the night ...? I stop. I go back to the computer and type the code into the special box. I click on a Russian beauty, she only does GFE and it's easy to see why. Her reviews are amazing, she must be working non-stop. One of her clients, Captain ——, has left her a very long review. He describes what a kind and loving girl this Russian beauty is. How tender she is when they hold hands, stroll together, how complimentary she is about his cooking. He talks at length about holding her at night, how he doesn't want to leave her in the mornings. He often has to get up very early for business flights and the thought of leaving her makes him very sad, so sad he sometimes cries. If he has to pick one of her best features, it's how she always goes and gets him his favourite Starbucks – without being asked – at the train station. When he's not looking, she'll go over and get it and give it to him with a kiss on the cheek. That makes him cry too. When he gets on the train, staring at the Starbucks cup, he thinks about how much he's going to miss her and what she means to him. Wow. It says here the Russian beauty speaks four languages, is trained in ballet and has a PhD in political sciences. Luckily she's also available for foreign travel.

I scroll through some of the other profiles. Each girl has a blurb.

Sonya: Sexy and sweet, can adapt to any situation.

Natalie: Huge brown eyes are hypnotic and her smile puts you at ease.

Scarlett: Seduces with the mind and the body and wants to know what makes men tick. A charming and cultured young lady who wouldn't look out of place on even the most powerful of gentlemen's arms.

Amie: An aesthetically exquisite young woman, having completed a master's in policy at a renowned American university, she's highly intelligent as well as intuitive and warm. African-American.

I can't help thinking how close these descriptions are to the one I have for my fictional escort. How similar to the descriptions of nearly every female part I've been sent. Ever.

I think a lot about these women. How long have they been escorting? The acronyms by their names, what they mean for them, on a nightly basis. I think about all the men with those strange usernames, the reviews they leave – like a TripAdvisor of bodies. I think about the photos of the women. Some of them with their faces blurred are only arms, legs, breasts, crotches, legs, hair, fingernails. All the parts that you'd be identified by in a morgue if your face was missing. I reel away from my own brain. I don't want to think about that. I don't ever want to think about these girls getting hurt. For all the tears Captain —— sheds over a Starbucks, there's an equal amount of other stuff. These agencies have legal jargon small-printed all over the place to protect themselves. The woman I talked to on the phone, the loving and protective people, they aren't there when the girls are alone in those rooms. When they travel abroad with these guys. These guys with their narcissistic usernames; Captain, Master, Machine. You paid a woman a grand and a half to hold your hand while you slept. What's the other side of your spectrum?

The next night, I call back. I decide to call myself Blue.

'Hey, darling, I was hoping you'd call again. You've got such a beautiful voice.'

'Say I was to come in? What would happen, what would I have to do?'

'Well, you would come into our offices. We've got a lovely photographer here who's lovely. OK? Then when you start earning, that's when lots of the girls get their professional photos done.'

We'd also talk about the things I felt comfortable doing.

'Do you have any experience?'

'No. No, I don't.'

She makes everything seem so easy. She'd take care of everything. She wants all her girls to feel safe. At home. There's a detail I need for the scene and so I ask.

'How do the girls – get paid? Is it still cash?'

'Yes, cash is a possibility. Lots of our girls nowadays have their own card machines though. They're very cheap to get hold of and it makes things a lot smoother, especially with the larger amounts.'

I tell her that I'm still thinking about things, that I was up unitl the wee hours reading the reviews. I'm still nervous. She tells me it's easy money. Nearly all her girls are doing it to put themselves through school.

'I'm good at spotting the damage.'

No damaged girls on her watch. Only the classy and the strong.

'If you've read the reviews you can see that for yourself.'

'Absolutely. Night night.'

'Not night night for me! Another coffee and I'll be all right. Goodnight, darling.'

I can't stop reading what Captain —— wrote.

I call back the next night just to chat.

'Sorry, what's your name? I never asked.'

'No one needs to know my name. It's Joan. What's yours?'

This feels like deep water.

'It's – Blue.'

'I like that, darling, I really like that. You should come and meet me.'

It's an open invitation to the most immersive research. But as committed as I am to doing all these women justice, this is a safe enough distance and I can tell that Joan is glad of the company.

'Start out on GFE. You've got such a soft, calming voice, it'd work well. I'd look after you. I'd look after you.'

'We'll see.'

I think it's the end of this now.

'Thanks so much for talking to me.'

'No worries, darling, call me back any time.'

The day of the shoot and I have a notebook overflowing for Blue. I've made her up out of all the women I've been familiarising myself with online. And all the men. And Joan. Despite there being no script, I've got a history for her, a future. Blue is twenty-three, same age as me. She's confident, not clearly 'damaged', but an abusive step-uncle altered her relationship to sex forever. After leaving home, she excelled at college, worked hard to find money to travel and got a place at university. With a scholarship she got her degree in French. But on leaving university she wanted to continue her travels, find her own apartment, think about even higher education. A friend had got into high-class escorting and introduced Blue to the kindly woman who ran the agency. They hit it off, she saw something in Blue. Knew she could make big money. After a while of doing the Girlfriend Experience, Blue grew tired of the needy older men. Their tears repulsed her. Their sagging skin made her feel close to death. Dinner and sex was easier, more detached. She travelled. And suddenly she found she was one of the top-earning escorts at the agency. Now, she doesn't have to work as much, she can choose her hours, cut down her client list to what suits her and plan her future.

> Young, sexy, exotic and beautiful. Blue is the perfect companion for any high-flyer. Her big brown eyes and warm smile make you feel at home, while her love of culture and languages makes her the ultimate international escort. The epitome of class with a natural 'girlfriend' quality too. Don't hesitate, her weekly hours are limited.

In my trailer, my costume is laid out. Stockings, suspender belt, suspenders, lace panties, bra, raincoat, bag. There we have it. In the make-up chair they put long flowing extensions into my hair; they feel too long for Blue – more stripper than the high-class French-speaking escort I've built up in my mind. Maybe Blue wears her hair long for special clients. I've never put on suspenders. I'm not sure what I'm doing. I imagine Blue nervous on her first job as I snap them into place. The kindly woman from the agency making a gift of expensive lingerie for her first booking, perhaps. The delicate fibre of the stockings on skin – I'm naturally clumsy and don't tend to wear anything below 60-denier so this takes effort. The belt pulls me in in places I've never seen on my body before. It cuts my stomach off from my hips. The suspenders are like a facelift for the thighs. I'm not so sure about the way they strap my bottom up, it feels like being pushed along by your arse constantly. The bra is beautiful, a dense black lace that looks too expensive to put underneath clothes. When I put the heels on and pull the raincoat around me – it's the missing piece of the jigsaw – I pick at some fruit, some grapes, stroke my long ponytail. Then it dawns on me, I've got to do this. I've got to do this in front of a room full of people, in front of a camera, and soon. The coolness of Blue drops away, my solar plexus drops down past the suspender belt. I'm me. I'm *so* me.

Walking to set and I'm clinging to my handbag, trying to use the height of the heels to give me some swagger. Try and stay in character. I think about the items in my handbag – I carefully packed things that would help me stay connected to Blue. You can tell a lot about a person by what they carry with them.

Softmints – packet twisted at the top.

Tissues – two used as lipstick blots.

Lipstick – Candy Rain.

Nail polish – Jeopardy, a purple-black.

Phone.

Purse – gold leather.

Pen – no lid.

We get to a glass-fronted building in a nice part of town – it's so tall you can see clouds reflected in it. I walk up the escalator. The director meets me, whispers so as not to break the atmosphere.

'You really look the part.'

The props person taps me on the shoulder, gives me the card machine I requested ahead of time. A tribute to Joan. The final detail. It goes in the bag. The cameras roll. I'm sent up in a lift, told by an assistant director to press floor 22. As soon as the button lights up, I want out. I'm not cut out for this. Any of it. The pretending of it. I'm carrying myself, I'm carrying Blue, I've got all those women from those sites with me. I want better for all of us. I'd rather be punching the businessman in the face than pretending to want to service his every need.

'It's just acting,' I whisper to myself. The doors open and there's the famous actor playing the horny businessman. He's already deep in character. The camera is behind him, on *me*. I have to jump in. I ask for payment up front as Blue would do. He obliges, putting his card in my machine and typing in his pin. The machine works! To my utter surprise and relief it starts to print a receipt! Would you look at that? I'm a pro. I tear it off and stuff it in his pocket without breaking eye contact. I ask where we should go to 'talk'. Discretion is key with high-profile clients. We walk into the office. The camera follows. It's completely made of glass; when my eyes adjust the London skyline is totally visible from every angle. Wow. Blue isn't impressed. I'd like to press my face up against the glass. Blue acts cool and tosses her ponytail over her shoulder. He offers her a drink. She declines. He offers her a line. She declines. Always decline drink or drugs on a booking. Unless that's part of your package. In and out is preferable on private calls like this. I ask about him, what he's been up to, about the office, the skyline. That's Blue's approachability factor. He wants to get straight down to it. Oh God. *I* panic. Blue is in control. She tosses her ponytail over her other shoulder and asks him to de-robe her. I pull clumsily at the too-tight knot I've made in the trench-coat belt. Blue laughs it off with her girl-next-door ease. The knot melts and falls away from her fingers. *I* take a deep breath. Think about the camera, my strapped-up arse captured for eternity on-screen. *She* thinks about the money, *her* future. I'm standing there in my 'costume', expensive lace making my nipples itch, alluring smile plastered on, lips twitching. Blue moves her head gracefully when the businessman comes in for the kiss. No kissing unless it's pre-arranged. The sign of an expert. I meanwhile, need to get my breath back. Things move to the sofa and the camera follows. The famous actor moves his hands all over me. I look at the ceiling. It's acting, we both tell ourselves. After a while there doesn't feel like much else within the realms of improvised drama that we can do besides actually having intercourse.

'*Ils ne vous payent pas assez, chérie.*'

They aren't paying you enough, darling, Blue whispers in my ear. Famous actor calls time on the scene. He can do that.

'We only need to go once more for angles.'

The director helps me on with my coat. One more time with feeling. I can do that. I can remove myself more this time. And every time. Like Blue. So we can protect ourselves. For our *future*.

INT. COFFEE SHOP, HIGH STREET.
AFTERNOON.

The cafe, downstairs from ACTRESS's flat,
is family-run. The simple decor fights
with the all-black exteriors of the
gentrified competition.

ACTRESS sits across from DAD. They nurse
two cups of tea. DAD looks concerned.

> DAD
>
> It's nice to be able to ask for a cup
> of tea without too many options.

> ACTRESS
>
> Tea doesn't just mean tea any more.
> It's decaf, herbal — bubble.

> DAD
>
> Too much choice. Is this too much for
> you? Being in here?

> ACTRESS
>
> Dad, I'm not agoraphobic.

> DAD
>
> I just thought you were working a
> lot.

                    ACTRESS
I am, working a lot.

                      DAD
So you feel OK being outside?

                    ACTRESS
This is downstairs from my
house, it's hardly outside,
it's just - downstairs. It's
practically the living room.
But yes, I feel OK.

                      DAD
What's going on then? Should we
worry? You look a little pale.
You're not losing weight, so
that's - a good -

                    ACTRESS
Now I feel awesome! Thanks! Fixed.

                      DAD
I always thought you put too much
pressure on yourself.

                    ACTRESS
Dad . . .

                      144

DAD

You put too much pressure on
yourself. Even when you were a girl.

ACTRESS

I'm fine.

DAD

It was a dream of yours, we just
supported. Should we have taken more
of an active role?

ACTRESS

Like what, be my agent?

DAD

OK.

ACTRESS

It was my choice, it still is.
There's nothing to be sorry for.
I'm OK. It's just — I don't know.
Do you think you can outgrow your
dreams maybe?

DAD

Your dreams are allowed to change.

ACTRESS

I might be trapped in a dream. It's
not a job any more. I don't know.
There's no line. I don't know where
it ends and I start.

DAD

Well, that's no good. You need to
cultivate yourself too. Look after
yourself.

ACTRESS

I know! But ... Did you know that
I haven't been able to dye my hair,
not once? In my life?

DAD

I've never noticed, no. I mean,
you didn't dye it green or pink
or anything like your boyfriends,
thank God.

ACTRESS

Exactly! I've wanted to dye my hair
green or pink or yellow or purple or
even black for goodness' sake and
I haven't been able to! Because of
work. I've had to stay in character —
forever.

                         DAD

You've cut your hair for roles,
you've got it very short now.

                        ACTRESS

I know, that's an exception. But it
was for *work.* It's someone else's
hair. It was for a character. This
hair isn't mine.

                         DAD

Isn't it? Looks so real.

                        ACTRESS

No, it's MINE, it's just not - mine.
It belongs to another woman, I'm just
looking after it for her until the
next one comes along.

                         DAD

REALLY?

                        ACTRESS

Dad, please get the metaphor here.
The hair is mine, it's attached to
my head, it just doesn't feel like
I own it. Even my wardrobe - not
that I've been modelling a vast
array of stuff recently. Leggings.

But I look in my wardrobe and I see
clothes that belong to other women.
I look in my wardrobe and I can't
see anything that belongs to me. I
should be able to go in my wardrobe
and find one item of clothing that
brings me back to myself. I bought
it, all, but none of it's for me.
There's white starched shirts and
blazers that belong to sexy, ball-
busting lawyers, and belly tops for
fun but occasionally suicidal best
friends, black polo-neck jumpers
for trainee policewomen, a torn
smock for an escaped slave. How
am I supposed to go clubbing in
that?

                    DAD
You go clubbing, do you?

                  ACTRESS
                  (*sighs*)
No. There's all these women, in the
wardrobe. I ran out of space.

                    DAD
Are we still in the metaphorical
realm?

ACTRESS
Well, yes! But also no.

DAD
Are you drinking too much?

ACTRESS
DAD!

DAD
Sorry, I think I understand. I do.
I'm just worried about you.

ACTRESS
It's OK. I'm OK. I just need some
time to —

They take sips.

DAD
Your hair will grow.

CUT TO:

Character: Rachael, late 20s.
Breakdown: Exotic beauty with a
questionable past. Lead.
Project: TV movie/international.

My hair isn't growing and I need a job to pay my rent. Versatility is apparently just – long hair. I draw eye level with the genderless heads in my local hair shop.

There's mid-length poker-straight. This will be good for: kindly policewomen/detectives with steely bedside manner/scientists with a hidden agenda/ headstrong junior doctors/office bitches and musical ingénues.

There's a mid-length one with a wave. This will be perfect for comedy girl next door/clumsy romantic co-lead/unintimidating best friend of colour in a romcom/supernatural college and high school projects.

There's a thick brown one with blonde highlights. This will carry me through the Latin spectrum – sassy Puerto Rican girls with one line in American house-party scenes/Mexican younger sisters trying to get their brothers to leave street gangs/sassy Latina wife with gold-digging advances on older Caucasian husband – comedy and drama.

A tightly curled black one with orange highlights – I'll take this to carry me effortlessly through all the delineations of the African diaspora with non-speaking roles/sassy girls who run their own salons/the drug mule who goes down for life/the convict surviving to tell her story/vulnerable women both volatile and shy/social workers who break the rules/prison security with attitude/checkout girls with hearts of gold/talented singers with abusive managers.

There's a really long blonde one streaked with pink and another with red. It's a subtle delineation, but red will work for crack whores/girls from the wrong side of the tracks trying to make good/supporting roles in films about boxers or rappers. The pink will be for single mothers trying their very best/bisexual neighbours/strippers going to night school/psycho girlfriends.

Then there's a short high-shine pony with lots of bounce, not what I'd naturally be drawn to but I can use this for a *lot*. Cancer survivors and computer whizz-kids/hot waitresses in a recurring role/outsiders in high school films about witchcraft/kooky artists in indie films or next-door neighbours in bigger-budget movies/female soccer hopefuls under 20/nannies and babysitters with no agenda/closet lesbian best friends/tomboys who get a date to the dance/ageless runaways in low-budget features/all-star students at the centre of rape investigations.

Before I know it my basket is full. It looks like evidence from a crime scene. I feel like Jack the Ripper with mementos of my latest victims.

'Why don't you get a weave? Good hair here.'

'I'm OK with the wigs.'

'Weave is good for you when you use good hair.'

The man behind the counter points me towards the section of the shop dedicated to human hair as opposed to the synthetic variety I'm stroking. I look at the prices. Buying human hair is like buying gold.

'I need something cheap.'

'You want to style? Heat style?'

'Possibly.'

Without much English, he shakes his head and does a detailed mime of my head bursting into flames, complete with my screaming for him to call the ambulance and the fire brigade.

'This? All ethical.'

He starts a well-rehearsed script about how the hair is sourced naturally or donated and I have to cut him short before he puts me off with blatant lies. He holds some hair up to my face and pulls a mirror out from under the counter. The hair – still half in plastic – droops, dead at the root over my eye. I imagine this woman, the woman whose hair I have against my face. Did she shave her head for a new beginning? I imagine her running her fingers over the shorn clumps of what's left. *Did* she give it willingly? It *is* a perfect match. I can't think about this any more. I pay for it, whispering a small prayer.

I take the hair to an address just outside London. A friend has recommended I see her 'weave woman'; she gives me the address like she's giving me the code to a vault where the Queen keeps her jewels.

'She's the best around and so quick, you won't believe.'

Weaves can take up your whole day; it's less an exercise in beauty, more in endurance of the human spirit. A little girl answers the door once I reach the given coordinates. She opens it just wide enough for a suspicious eye. What is this, a hair speakeasy? I feel like there's a password I should know, which the little girl won't let me in without.

'I'm here for a chat with your mum about something.'

'She's not my mum.'

She doesn't blink.

'A friend sent me.'

The door doesn't move even a centimetre.

'I'm here for a weave.'

She waits until I reach into the bag and display the evidence.

She lets the chain off and I head upstairs.

Weave woman has a name, Sharmian. She embraces me like an old friend, and when I tell her it's my first time, she pinches my ribs like a virgin.

'Trust me, you'll be fine.'

She smiles and cleans up the chair for me to sit on. She takes my packets of hair and winks, looks impressed. I relax. She unpacks the hair, it unravels – endlessly. I imagine the scalping knife, the hair falling in perfect rings like the skin of an apple.

'I didn't know how much to get.'

'This will be perfect. You want a fringe too, bangs?'

'Whatever you think.'

'I think that would suit you well.'

'Why is there so much hair?'

She can see I've been carrying a weight.

'Don't worry. I always bless the hair before using it.' She smiles.

I smile now. We place our hands over it and close our eyes, as she leads me in her ritual.

'For what has been sacrificed, may we be truly thankful. Amen.'

With that, the needle threads past my scalp. She tells me stories of her days as a hairdresser to West Africa's elite. Now she prefers the anonymous life, weaving on her own terms. When I drift off, she expertly sews around my lolling head. Late afternoon turns to night, and when we're done, I look like someone else.

Maybe it's the hair, the fringe, maybe it's the blessing, but it's not long before I land something new. A leading role in something I'm really passionate about. I'm counting my blessings and taking my weave maintenance seriously. Like any invasive operation, you have to keep up with the aftercare.

Halfway through the job, my make-up artist whispers in my ear discreetly.

'Do you want me to cover your greys?'

Greys? I don't have any greys. The make-up artist uses a fine-tooth comb to lift and separate my hair in the mirror, showing me clearly defined chunks of grey hair.

'Oh my God.'

'It happens to us all, no bother.'

'No.'

I show her.

'Look. My hair ends here.'

She runs her hands along the woven tracks.

'How is that even possible?'

She continues with the fine-tooth comb.

The weave is going grey at the root.

Maybe they were there when I bought it? I knew the guy behind the counter seemed overly keen to sell. I feel sick. The image of the bald woman plays again, the knife. Is she using me as a host? Is she somewhere in the world worrying her heart out? Traumatised by hair theft? But we ran it through our hands, blessed it from root to tip. That should have expelled any poltergeists. Time is tight, we cover the greys and I head to set. But I can *feel* them. All day. The more I bring the character to life, the more the hair lives – on me.

At home, the greys seem to have doubled when I wash the root spray out. I tweeze the greys, one by one they ping out of their synthetic edging. Before I know it, the sink is full. Can I get the weave cut out and return it somehow? I need to find this woman. The woman who sacrificed her hair. The hair is from Brazil. I know that much, it says so on the packet. It's where hair 'is best' according to that fucking hair farmer. If the hair is alive, maybe it could lead me to her? I repeat the blessing and hope for a sign. Nothing. I wash the greys down the plughole. As I watch the running water, I imagine finding her, kneeling by a stream as she watches the tourist boats sail by. I could kneel beside her, unwrap the hair from the paper I've lovingly carried across oceans, and hand it back. I could show her where it was going grey, she wouldn't have known. There could be an unspoken understanding between us, as women, that I never meant to play a part in her sadness, her stress. Her abuse. What's the universal sign for acting gig? Not that I'd expect to justify it. I hope she'll want to understand. I could offer to lightly sponge her back in the stream. She could dip me under the water. We could start again.

INT. BEDROOM, BOY'S HOUSE. NIGHT.

ACTRESS *pushes the door open
tentatively.* BOY *stirs, stares down the
shaft of light.* ACTRESS *is silhouetted
like a serial killer in a movie.*

They stare at each other for a time.

> BOY
>
> You could have given me a heart
> attack.

> ACTRESS
>
> I kept my key.

> BOY
>
> I knew it. How often have you been
> letting yourself in?

> ACTRESS
>
> What? That's ridicu—

> BOY
>
> How many times?

Pause.

                    ACTRESS
Sometimes for a bath.

                     BOY
Is that why you're here?

                    ACTRESS
No.

                     BOY
Are you in pyjamas?

                    ACTRESS
Absolutely not.

ACTRESS *walks over to the bed, sits
softly on the duvet. It makes a gentle
sound, like a long sigh, as the air
leaves it.* BOY *puts the bedside light
on, puts a T-shirt on.*

                    ACTRESS
I wanted to talk about love.

BOY *puts his head in his hands.*

                    BOY
I'm not sure I can do this.

                  ACTRESS
Wait, wait, wait.

                    BOY
It's taken forever to even feel
vaguely normal, since —

                  ACTRESS
I know! I know. I'm not dead inside!

Silence.

                  ACTRESS
Why aren't you saying anything? You
think I'm dead inside, don't you?

                    BOY
No.

                  ACTRESS
Your silence speaks volumes. Good
evening.

                    BOY
Wait! That's not what I was thinking!
But . . .

                    ACTRESS
    But? There's a but? Good evening.

ACTRESS *stands to leave.*

                     BOY
    You're the one here in the middle of
    the night!

She sits again, the same soft sigh.

                    ACTRESS
    Do you still think about me?

                     BOY
    (*with both hands gripping his hair*)
    You know I do.

                    ACTRESS
    When you do, is it with words or
    pictures?

                     BOY
    What?

                    ACTRESS
    Do you think about me with words or
    pictures?

                    BOY

I can't believe I'm — (*sigh*) — both.
I suppose. Yeah. Both. There's
memories made up of both. Words
sometimes, I don't know.

                  ACTRESS

Huh. *(Pause.)*
Did you love me?

                    BOY

What is this? Yes! Of course I did,
you know I did!

                  ACTRESS

I don't! And I want to. I need to
know what that felt like. Can you
describe it? Physically?

                    BOY

You don't know? You broke in to tell
me you never loved me and ask me to
describe what that might have felt
like?

                  ACTRESS

I have a *key*. It's not breaking
in when you have a key.
I did, I did love you.

                    BOY

What are you doing? This isn't a
game.

                  ACTRESS

I need you to tell me what it felt
like. Because, I've pretended to
love a lot of people.

                    BOY

What is this?

                  ACTRESS

I could list them? It's a lot. And
they've pretended to love me. Why
would we be capable of anything
different? Why would you think I'd
be capable of anything but that?
Pretend?

                    BOY

I know you loved me. Because
I loved you.

                  ACTRESS

Is that your answer then? Love is
the other person loving you?

                    BOY
    I suppose. It's just like a bath.

He smiles. She smiles.

Silence.

                  ACTRESS
    I feel so hollow sometimes. Did
    you ever feel that? I can see my
    arms moving, my legs, I can hear my
    own voice echo in my throat, I can
    hear the words. But I don't feel —
    anything. I think that's why. That's
    what happened — here. With us.

                    BOY
    You're saying you were acting,
    constantly? For years?

                  ACTRESS
    No!

Silence.

                    BOY
    I have to sleep. This isn't a film,
    we're not onstage. This is my life.

                    ACTRESS
    Mine too! I'm trying to communicate
    to you that I'm suffering from a
    dissociative malady and I can't
    find the exit!

Silence.

                      BOY
    Well, if this is a play, I'd like a
    better part next time.

                    ACTRESS
    That is a GREAT line.

                      BOY
    I knew I should have taken half a
    Valium tonight.

A long silence.

                    ACTRESS
    Can you stroke my hair for a second?
    Just to see if I can feel it?

                                    CUT TO:

Character: Viv, any age.
Breakdown: Fearless outsider.
Project: Original comedy/TV.
Notes from casting: Please ignore where
it's marked Vincent in the script,
this is now a female role. Submit all
ethnicities.

The air of this day is so nice. Working in summer is so sweet. The day extends out in front of me, a lovely bed of grass. I feel in step. Everyone feels happier. It's warm. I'm enjoying work. A long telly job, a comedy, that takes the pressure off making rent for once. I feel safe, I feel loved, I feel like I'm among family. It's a great cast who feel like instant lifelong friends. We laugh from morning until night, shouldn't be called a job really.

We're being driven to work when I get a phone call. In the car. It's one of those phone calls that collapses everything. I've got an aunt, a close aunt, who's been ill for a long while. The cancer's ended up in her blood and bones. When the phone rings and it's Mum – the green grass of the day yellows. Mum can barely use her phone. It's a pleasure to receive the texts she sends all in upper case, like she's shouting love at me, but if she's calling, if she's using her credit, all can't be well. I let it ring out. She calls again. When I put the phone on silent, everyone in the car wants to know if it's a boy I'm jilting. I tell them it is. The phone vibrates. I tell them he wants me bad. Smile. The grass dies as the car drives me to work.

I sit in my trailer, in our little trailer park. I sit and look at the missed calls from Mummy New Mob. I have five minutes before I have to be in the make-up chair and an hour before going on camera. I can call back and ask a question I don't want the answer to, or I can pretend none of this is happening and get my face done. I call. I have to call because a fire is starting in my kidneys. My whole body knows I'm lying, even if my friends don't.

The cancer started in her breasts, but her spirit and the nurses beat it. When we talked on Skype, she and her kids were more concerned with what ice-cream flavour to choose than anything else. Her voice was weak. I ignored it. It's emotion, she's been through a lot. I never thought it was her body failing again. When they tell you it's in the blood, you start making your peace. But I don't think I ever did. I used that unshakeable hope, the kind reserved for the righteous and religious. The hope of the dying themselves.

When I get through to Mummy New Mob, all my fears cave in on my face, because I hear her voice and I know, the tears come right away. I had hoped with all the hope that it's possible for one body to have, and I was wrong. It's happened. What's the time? I look at the clock. This is what time it is when our lives change for ever. It's when I look at the clock that I'm hit with the irreversibility of everything. The youngest sibling on my mum's side has gone. My auntie, more like a second mum to me, has gone. The light outside is white as Mum talks about arrangements, she needs to skate quickly past this grief that could stop time. I watch the clock tick down. See the digital time and date display on my phone. I always thought it was black that digital clock, but now I realise it's the darkest of browns. It's time to get make-up done, time to go to work, and my eyes are red balloons in my face and her body is making its way back from New York and I want to know the name of every child without a mother. But I also want to answer the door, have a coffee, go to work, be normal. I can't let the nuclear grief out in this little cabin, can't go home. I don't know what would happen if I tried to board a train now, I can't imagine buying a ticket and a small fruit salad. I've got the details now, Mum needs to go and make more calls, I've told the person at the trailer door that I'm on my way, and I don't know who hung up first but the line is quiet and the phone's put itself to sleep. The days are getting hotter, so I have sunglasses. Where? On my head. Yes. I stopped feeling them. I slide them down. Hide inside the shade of them. Let the greenish black of the lenses stain the room. I look at the table. The chair. The drawer. The window. My feet. The door handle.

The lights in the make-up bus are fluorescent and burn through my coolness. I raise my hand, the one that isn't holding the coffee cup, to shield myself and my friend, my colleague who's sat in one of the make-up chairs, laughs. It looks like I have an almighty hangover. Shades on, caffeine fix, light sensitivity, trembling hand. I don't laugh and that makes her laugh more. My blank face intensifies what she imagines. It doesn't upset me, the laughter. I like it. I could hide behind it if my brain wasn't so short-circuited. I could laugh along and make up a story about how late I got in last night. Who I might have kicked out of my bed. Instead of telling the truth.

I'm tired, the most tired I've ever been, and so can only tell the truth.

'My auntie died. Please don't be nice to me, I'll cry.'

Everyone is quiet. They manage niceness without setting me off. Nice that doesn't cross the boundary of nice. Not the kind of nice that will take me into the big heaving noises I've never made before, the kind of crying which must be reserved for later, when I'm home. Or in the train toilet. The wonderful woman doing my make-up conceals and pencils around the redness, powders out any fresh tears that roll down. I put my head back, all the way back in the chair, and she lets me close my eyes as she creates a new character on my face. I realise I've probably spent more hours of my life in a make-up chair than with members of my family. She's gentle and low-key with my hair, creates a simple style. Lets it wash over me. This strange thing of making up an artist who is a shell. When you willingly have your hair and make-up done, it's fun. Your face takes the creams and the blushes well, your lips take the lipstick, your face moves into the shape of the colours and softens and hardens in the places it needs to, to create the new you. Putting make-up on when you're deep in grief is something quite different. Your face doesn't want to move or bend or be any shape other than the shape of mourning. It doesn't want to yield to colour, I can see it, my face is literally *drinking* the colour in, draining it, getting rid. It wants and needs to be washed out and pale, ashen and yellow. The eyeliner on the waterlines of my eyes seems to be sitting an inch or so away from my face. It hasn't stuck. My eyelashes have gone sideways with the mascara, like they're attempting to leave my face. The lipstick has dried in place, the moisture in my lips has disappeared and the dry skin flakes the colour off. Make-up needs the cooperation of your face. My face doesn't want to hide. It has to be seen, it's asking to be seen as it is. But I have to go to work. My job today is to make people laugh.

Parallel universes are 'a hypothetical self-contained reality co-existing with one's own'. I google it as I walk to the set. I need an explanation for what's happening. It's not an out-of-body experience, I google that too to make sure, which is 'an experience that typically involves a feeling of floating outside one's body and, in some cases, the feeling of perceiving one's physical body as if from a place outside one's body'. I'm not floating outside myself, I'm here. I'm here in a reality that isn't real but I am real and we are operating simultaneously. When I move my hand, I can see it's mine, it's my movement, my thought – but it also exists as someone else's. When I say hello to the rest of the cast and the crew, it's my voice. But when I hear it, it rings in two places, in the real world and in the self-contained reality. When I sit down in front of the camera, I'm aware it's a camera. I look down the lens and see the little upside-down rainbow reflection. My lines are bouncing off the walls of my head because that's what grief does, it makes the inside of your skull extra slippy. Anything temporary unsticks and only the long-term memories, like limpets, cling on for dear life. I'm thinking about almost nothing but those. They're often the simplest ones. Chinese takeaways, cinema trips, birthday parties. But when the moment comes the lines do come out of my mouth. I manage to make being a human believable, maybe even funny. That's my job today. The few people in the know squeeze my hand between takes and bring me cups of tea, shoot supportive laser beams out of their eyes from across the room. The real joke is, that I'm actually on fire today. It's the quickest and funniest I think I've been the entire shoot. I've managed to make the sadness fall down inside me, it pops down in a little secret lift and waits very patiently on the ground floor. The warmth comes up in my cheeks again and I can feel my make-up blending together at last. The hairs on my head stop sticking up, and smooth themselves down behind my ears and over one eye. Laughter is medicine for now. It's a powerful potion and its effects are quick. Little by little, angle by angle, the scene gets done. I've only got one today – a blessing. Days are long on this job. I can't say any more words that aren't my own today. At the end, everyone's happy. I've given a good performance. But the portal of the parallel universe stays open. It follows me, like the viewfinder on a gun. The duality stays and stays and stays. When my make-up comes off, when my costume comes off, when my own clothes go on and I look in the mirror at my own self – there's still me and alternate-reality me. I touch my face. I put my arms out to the side. I move my hips in a circle. Say my own name three times. It feels like me and *not* me. My movements feel self-conscious. Like I'm not in charge. Everything feels like it's happened before. Like I'm taking steps already trodden. Like I'm saying words already written. It feels like all of this is *for* someone. Someone who isn't me. Someone I know and don't know all at once. Someone who's watching. This lasts on the ride to the station, on the train. I eat my fruit salad in slow motion to try and trip the wires of the portal. Maybe I'm just on a delay, this might help sync me up.

When the funeral comes, me and myself are still beside ourselves – we put our make-up on. It freezes and seizes up in all the same places, same as the day I found out. Powder cakes on my forehead and the eyeliner pulls across my skin like Magic Marker on drywall. I watch my hands do my hair and feel them do up the zip of my dress. I marvel as they carefully roll up my tights without tearing them with my nails. When my chest heaves in the church, I can't believe I can get the tissues to reach my face. When my arms reach out to my aunt's young daughter, she smiles at me, tries to make *me* brave, and it's like it's happened before. At the graveside when the animal sound lurches out of my ribcage, my brain is taking notes. 'Yes, that sounded like an animal. Not sure which one. Come back to it later.' There isn't a single thing that doesn't feel like it's being commented upon somewhere, somehow. When my legs give way at the sight of Grandmother's grief, when I kneel at the feet of her wheelchair, it all has that same feeling. I'm self-aware at every turn. I'm conscious of my dress being creased from the waist down from the car ride, my manicured hands. When I turn and look backwards at the open grave, I wonder if I'm *pretending* to be a woman in a sad film. A mourning woman, all in black, looking woefully backwards over her shoulder as the pallbearers lift the ropes over the dirt. I've never seen this particular film, but it feels like I have, and I was in it. I'm currently recreating it scene by scene.

The parallel universe lasts for a long time. The portal stays open for a long time. Except when my eyes open first thing in the morning and the thought of being awake is the only thought. Before my blurred vision focuses. Before I move any part of myself.

INT. THERAPIST'S OFFICE. DAY.

ACTRESS *sits. The leatherette squeaks as she moves.*

                    THERAPIST
          Being watched?

ACTRESS *squeaks to a comfy position.*

                    ACTRESS
          Most days I feel like a human woman
          walking down the street, pretending
          to be a human woman walking down the
          street.

                    THERAPIST
          Two different people?

                    ACTRESS
          No, no — I'm not, it's not a
          schizophrenic thing. It's like
          I'm — performing, but as — myself.
          I don't know how to turn it off.
          I can't brush my teeth, put lipstick
          on, get dressed, undress, have
          sex, take a shit, cry, read a
          book — without this nagging
          feeling that it's for someone

                    173

else's benefit. That I'm playing up to
an — audience.

                    THERAPIST
Who's in the audience?

                    ACTRESS
I don't know. I can't see them, but
they're there. Sometimes it feels
like just one person.

                    THERAPIST
Who's that person?

                    ACTRESS
I don't know. But they hold the
cards.

                    THERAPIST
How long has it felt this way? Do you
think?

                    ACTRESS
I feel like I've been in character my
whole life.

                    THERAPIST
Well, in a way you have.

ACTRESS

I started early, yeah.

THERAPIST

And you'd like that to stop?

ACTRESS

Yes. I would. I need it to. Everyone's
worried about me. I feel like whatever
it is I have might be preventing me
from accessing my real life. I'm not
in it, I'm not connected currently.
Days pass in bed.

THERAPIST

Good acting is so much about truth.
About connection?

ACTRESS

I believe that, I do. I've
experienced so much of that in my
career. I think I can connect, get it
all going, but — I think, maybe I've
connected until the connectivity is
gone? Truth feels mighty — objective.

THERAPIST

You have access to the power to
change your career.

ACTRESS

Yes. Ha, good point, why not just
stop? Here you go, there's the cash,
thanks for fixing me. Ha. No, it's
not so much even the acting any more.
The craft, the working, it has its
good points. It's the performing. It
doesn't turn off. (*Pause.*)
Why won't it turn off?

THERAPIST

You must have liked it at one time?
Pretending to be other people? Part
of that is fun, escape?

ACTRESS

I think it was at one time.

THERAPIST

When's the last time you remember
enjoying it?

ACTRESS

Um ... I can't, right now.

THERAPIST

What parts of your life do you think
you've, as you say, had trouble
accessing?

ACTRESS

It's ... it's love mainly, maybe,
mostly. Love. Yeah. I don't seem to
be able to love things — people —
properly.

THERAPIST

What does love properly look like?

ACTRESS

Alive? Feelings that go all the
way in, all the way down. Not
just, halfway. I feel like I'm
perpetually waiting for someone
to shout cut. Some scenes are
longer than others, some co-stars
more believable than others.
But ultimately, I need to
save myself for my other
performances.
So, does anyone truly get — me?
Maybe I've just stopped feeling —
anything. Or maybe I'm just feeling
everything? And that's, well, that's
just impossible.

ACTRESS *laughs at her own realisation.*

                    THERAPIST
Would you like some water?

                    ACTRESS
Yes, please.

THERAPIST *reaches for the glass decanter
on the table in front of them and pours
some water into a plastic cup. She hands
it to ACTRESS.*

                    ACTRESS
Thank you. Even holding this cup
feels ... I want to stop feeling
like a goldfish in a fucking bowl,
and I don't know whether I'd need
that even if the acting had never
happened. My earliest memory — here
you go — I'm jumping to my earliest
memory without you even asking,
that's what therapists ask in the
movies, isn't it? Well, mine is of
being about two. One or two, one
I think actually. I know that's
potentially too early to form memory,
but I did. I did. A neighbour had a
new camera and he came round to take
my portrait, a baby portrait. And, I
remember I was crawling around, quite

happily, on the carpet, chewing on an apple, dribble everywhere, but I remember being happy. Happy and free and just a big fat happy baby. And then my mum and dad came in and took the apple away and I remember my arm reaching up to get it, to get it back. But one of them put it on the side. Fair enough, it wasn't the first time fruit had been taken away half chewed, covered in carpet. I was on to the next thing, a Lego man nearby — I can attempt to eat him! So I was crawling at a pace towards Lego man when there was a flash. A flash of our neighbour's camera. When I turned, just to see what the flashing was — just exercising my big fat baby instinct — I saw this camera in my face and a strange man at the other end of it. And, as you might expect, I found myself staring directly down the lens. I remember the rainbow reflection in that big black hole. The little curved upside-down rainbow. It flashed again, and to be honest, I found it annoying. My neighbour was making crazy faces at me, every time it flashed. But I

didn't take the bait. I wanted to
be left alone to cover my toys in
drool. It snapped and flashed again.
It was almost blinding. He was coming
closer. I was sitting perfectly still
by this point, totally despondent.
'Smile! Smile! Smile!' I remember him
saying. 'Come on, coochie coochie' or
something, I don't know. But I didn't
want to smile. 'You have a beautiful
smile!' I'm not smiling. I'm not
smiling, I thought. 'A beautiful
smile! That's it!' And I'm thinking,
Is this guy made of wood? I'm *not*
fucking smiling. But he wouldn't
leave me alone. He wanted that shot.
So, after a long time not smiling, I
smiled. I knew that's what would buy
me my freedom. I smiled this little
half-smile and that was it. He left
and I got my apple back. It was a
trade-off.
That's a legitimate memory. I have
the photo to prove it. I look like
the *Mona Lisa*, but more fucked off.
I feel like I'm making that contract
again every day.

Pause.

                    THERAPIST
Sometimes we can remember processed
emotion as though we experienced it
at the time.

                     ACTRESS
No. I was there. Like I'm here now.
Almost here.

                                  CUT TO:

Character: Cora, 20–30 yrs.
Description: Damaged beauty with a taste for murder.
Project: Stage/West End.

I'm onstage and I'm convinced I've started my period. Red patches are blooming in my costume, for all to see. Red drips of real blood are flowing from me, dripping a trail of shiny red ooze for the audience to follow with their eyes and gasp at. Point at. I'm not anywhere near my period. I'm in the tiny wonderland of being a normal temperature, my breasts fitting back into my shirts and my skin not feeling like the surface of a cheap waterbed. It's a calm oasis, the eggs feel like they're safely regenerating deep within the womb lining and, for a couple of weeks at least, I'll feel something resembling – balanced. So why? *Why* do I feel that blood running down my thighs and gathering in my toes?

No sooner have we started, than I – my character – have to strip down to underwear. I'm glad of it. Unlike much nudity onstage or screen, this is warranted and every bit earned. The character is exposed and vulnerable, it helps with the connection between me and the audience, and with the other character onstage. The underwear is white. Has to be. I've chosen it even though I haven't worn white underwear since the day I got my first period. White shorts, white jeans, white swimming costumes, white sofas – they only exist in memory now.

But even though white might not be right for me, it's right for my character. It's right for this woman, her life. She's a woman-child, an innocent. In her head, she lives in a pre-period world, her adult development arrested years ago by trauma. This isn't white underwear that is supposed to toe the boring 'virgin/whore' line, white satin cut into girlish shapes trimmed with adult lace. It's washed-out white-grey and sags in all the wrong places. It's real. This underwear belongs to a person, not a tired construct.

And when I take off my costume the first couple of nights, I'm exhilarated, I'm excited to remove the layers and strip down to the bare physical and emotional essentials. I don't feel gazed at and passive in a room full of strangers, I feel confrontational and alive. Apart from now. Right now. All that's falling apart. As soon as I undressed I felt a gush of blood. I look at my fellow actor, my eyes struck through with fear. Her eyes flicker, she thinks we've missed a cue.

I feel the blood spreading. I start to circle the stage with my back to the walls, changing weeks' worth of choreography. I try and walk in such a way that can hide the back of my pants from the audience and squeeze my pelvic floor to stem the flow. I can feel the blood escape my pants and start to run down my leg, so I suddenly find myself having to do a flamingo impression, much to the surprise of my colleague. I'm trying to scrape my foot up my inner thigh to rub it away before anyone sees it. I still seem to be getting lines out in the right order, despite hopping on one leg. What's starting to push me off centre is something in the audience – moving, fourth row or so, looks like there might be a small kerfuffle breaking out. Out of the corner of my eye, I'm sure I see a finger pointing. Someone is pointing right at me. They feel faint at the sight of my blood and are telling the ushers they want their money back. They're livid. The people who aren't trying to leave are whispering, telling them to wait until the interval. There is no interval! The sight of my menstrual blood is killing people and nearly the whole of the fifth row has emptied. I can see it. I angle myself to see the audience more clearly. There's no time to mouth an apology to my partner on the stage, I'm surprised she hasn't seen the exodus of the fifth row and isn't trying, like me, to alter her own blocking to get a better view of what's going on. I move further and further downstage, more and more out of the play we've painstakingly rehearsed. My lines float out of my mouth and over my head, completely disconnected from my body. My pelvic floor contracts with each step. Instead of keeping the flow in, it's now acting as a pump action, pumping the blood like fresh water out of a well. Out of me. I'm too scared to look down and see the red tsunami I'm wading through. At the edge of the stage, I jut out my neck and squint against the lights. I keep pushing my lines out as my eyes adjust; when the haze dissipates, I see the fifth row is intact – packed from end to end with attentive audience members. The people I initially thought were trying to escape are actually a friendly-looking older couple holding large hats in their laps. Perhaps one of the hats was blown upwards on the particularly aggressive air conditioning? It doesn't look like the audience have been disturbed at all. Maybe they don't even think this river of blood belongs to me! Perhaps they think it's a clever theatrical device, a blood pouch in my knickers that's activated by an invisible thread. How long have I been gone? I need to get to my next cue, getting my clothes on again. I can wipe the blood on the inside of the black dress I wear next. I turn and give a wink to my fellow actress who has broken into a sweat trying to carry a departed me through the scene. As long as no one knows, I can get back on track. I reach down to grab my tights laid out on the floor, my first costume cue. Before I put them on, I'm going to use them like a wash mitt, rub them vigorously up my legs to get the last long drips and any remaining puddles. I let my next line take my gaze down to the floor to locate where I need to mop.

I look at my legs. No snaking red lines. There's no pool on the floor beneath me or anywhere else. I'm so shocked, I search at my crotch with my fingers. Dry. Not a drop. My colleague is eyeing me again. I owe her. I hit all my cues at double speed and make up for lost time.

Safely underneath the stage, I rip my tights down to my knees, pull the white knickers down too – which could be wrung out with sweat by now, nothing else. But the trickling, the dripping, the spilling? I grab the stage manager by the shoulders.

'I'm so sorry. I was convinced I'd started my period. That my costume, my whole underwear was soaked. The hopping, the changing up the blocking, I was convinced everyone could see.'

'Have you?'

'What?'

'Come on?'

'No, no I haven't. But I was convinced, I mean – I could feel ... You didn't see any audience members leaving, tonight? Did you?'

'No ... They're a good crowd actually.'

'Yeah, they are. They are.'

INT. LOCAL SUPERMARKET. DAY.

A *long mac over Teenage Mutant Ninja Turtles leggings,* ACTRESS *browses the breakfast pastries.* OLDER ACTRESS *approaches, carrying a box of wine.*

> OLDER ACTRESS
> It *is* you!

ACTRESS *turns, horrified to bump into anyone she knows. She plasters on a smile.*

> ACTRESS
> It's — *me!*

OLDER ACTRESS *gives* ACTRESS *a bear hug.*

> OLDER ACTRESS
> It's so nice when you bump into people you genuinely like. How are you?

> ACTRESS
> I'm well, really really really well.

> OLDER ACTRESS
> Been busy since the play? Working?

ACTRESS

Yep. Auditioning. Loads of —
exciting — stuff.
Are you well? You look — well.

OLDER ACTRESS

Argh! I'm haggard. We've been
shooting nights on this detective
drama, arse end of nowhere. Mustn't
moan though — since the kid I need
to take the work whatever, wherever.

ACTRESS

Sure.

OLDER ACTRESS

Within reason, though.

ACTRESS

Show no good?

OLDER ACTRESS

No, it's great. It's a great show,
great part. Just — after the shoot
last night, I'm not sure how much
of my face you're going to see.

ACTRESS

What?

                    OLDER ACTRESS
Well, the cameraman just kept
shooting, well, my breasts.

                       ACTRESS
What kind of crime was it?

                    OLDER ACTRESS
Haha! Well, a serial killer rapes me,
then asphyxiates me, leaves me in a
ditch. Classic.

                       ACTRESS
Classic.

                    OLDER ACTRESS
So, I'm in underwear, my head is in
this see-through bag with a noose
round it, and I'm doing my best
dead acting and I can just sense
that the camera isn't on my face. I
can't open my eyes obviously, but
I can just feel it. Anyway, then I
tell myself to stop being paranoid.
But when I finally get the bag off my
head and see some playback over the
producer's shoulder, there was my
bosom! Dripping in blood. Cut, end

of episode! Not sure it was how I
would have drummed up empathy with my
character, but hey-ho. Mustn't moan.

She laughs.

Silence.

                ACTRESS
My usual shop was out of croissants.

             OLDER ACTRESS
Things have been slow, I'm glad of
the work. Turning thirty felt like
being dead, work-wise, and having the
kid was the final nail in the coffin.
Are you —?

OLDER ACTRESS *makes a face, awkward.*

                ACTRESS
Dead?

             OLDER ACTRESS
Haha!

                ACTRESS
Just, yeah.

OLDER ACTRESS

These are the twilight years. You're
not an ingénue and you're not a
grandma, so — see ya!
Those casting age brackets don't
help!

*She jostles the wine box, cups her hands
to mime a pair of brackets, she pushes
them apart.*

OLDER ACTRESS

They're getting wider! Thirty-
plus, that's a thing now. I went in
for something, something I really
wanted. It said 'thirties-plus' on
the breakdown. I thought I nailed the
audition, my agent calls and tells me
it's gone to an actress I know for
a fact is nearly sixty! I hope my
ninety-seven-year-old grandma doesn't
take up acting, we'll be competing
for the same roles. She doesn't have
as good boobs as me, thank goodness.

CUT TO:

Character: Tamala the Witch Doctor,
30—40 yrs.
Breakdown: A rural community are
targeted by religious vigilantes when
women come forward with testimonies of
abuse.
Project: Period drama.
Notes from casting: Full-frontal nudity
required. Only submit actresses prepared
to sign a nudity clause.

'Areola, no nipple?'

My agent reads the suggested provisos for my nudity clause with a level of seriousness absolutely warranted by the nature of this contract, but I find myself stifling childish laughter. I imagine Areola and Nipple as two animated friends, like Pooh and Piglet. One small and energetic, the other slow and oafish.

'Areola, no nipple. What does that actually mean?'

'It means, on camera, they're allowed to show your areola, but not your nipple.'

I slide my hand under my T-shirt and cup my breast, ponder the span of my areola in proportion to my nipple. A large cup of hot chocolate with a single mini marshmallow?

'If they can separate the two, agreed.'

'Side boob no frontal?'

I like my side boobs.

'Sounds good. Will help keep the nipples out of the picture.'

I move my hand round the cup to my side boob, press my whole palm against it. I imagine the reviews for the show should these provisos be accepted.

The use of areola in this female-led historical thriller was gratuitous and utterly inexplicable. Historical accuracy was clearly sidelined to also incorporate an inordinate amount of the actress's side boob, which had clearly been enhanced for effect using a cosmetic glitter gel completely at odds with the period.

'How do you feel about sitting or standing naked?'

This clause will protect me from any nudity in motion – running, skipping, undulating generally in any way.

'I feel good about it,' I say without thinking. My mind is numbing over. This isn't funny any more. Do I feel good? I slip my hand out from under my bra. How am I to attempt to touch the human soul if my main focus is keeping all the parts of my anatomy that are supposed to go together separate?

'Now, this isn't one we're happy about.'

It's still going.

'Vagina is non-negotiable.'

'Huh.'

I like to think my vagina has always been non-negotiable.

'*But* vagina no pubic hair is on the table.'

And now I'm flooded with images of bald vaginas on tables. They take the form of small plucked chickens, oiled and ready to be seasoned.

'So, I have to agree to show my vagina, but I *don't* have to show my pubic hair? I'm not sure I'm following the logic any more.'

'There isn't much, lots of these will be struck off, everyone's just trying to do their best to protect you right now.'

At this point I think I give up on the work I was doing on the *inner* world of a religious woman fighting for survival and abandoning the Church in the seventeenth century, and try and connect to the kind of wax she might have. Would she have the money or inclination for a full Hollywood?

'Don't worry, I think that's one you can talk through with the director on the day, should it come to it.'

'Yes, well, exactly.'

Great, I've always wanted to relive a moment as awkward as the day I told my father I'd started menstruating.

'Full behind is also non-negotiable. There's some wording I can employ that could mean only side bottom and no close-ups.'

A close-up of my full behind? Even the people who might *want* to see that would change their minds at the harsh reality, surely?

'Some wording to avoid that would be great. At all costs.'

At this point, I'd rather have my whole vagina shown as forensically as possible. Have a camera attached to the end of one of those lubed-up devices they carry out smear tests with. In fact, I now want to do the whole project naked *and* running, with scissors, scissors that I clearly don't use to cut the pubic hair that grows down past my inner thighs. From a distance I could be wearing cycling shorts.

'A body double is also an option if it's decided that a scene warrants full nudity.'

'So, a nudity clause so I don't have to be nude, but if I do have to be nude – I can actually exercise my right to use someone else entirely?'

'The logic is misty, at best.'

I've had a stunt double before but never a body double. My stunt doubles are always men, because of my being so tall. It's strange handing the scene you were trying to bring as much emotional truth to as possible to a man in full 'you' drag then watching him being beaten or thrown down some stairs. We usually have a good laugh between takes as we tag each other in and out of the scene. We take photos in our matching costumes. All a bit of fun. But to be sat in a chair, having a cup of tea on a break from shooting, next to the woman hired to play my privates? This isn't a situation I've ever even dreamed of.

Will she have to shadow me? Like an understudy? A bum-erstudy? Watch how my buttocks move, how they react to certain atmospheres? How does she feel about playing my – parts? Is she an actress? If she is, why doesn't she want to speak? Is she happy letting her areola do the talking? Is this a part-time thing while she pursues other interests? I imagine *her* full behind in a close-up. I'm sure it's like two peach halves slipped from a can, any imperfections glazed over with syrup. It slides effortlessly in its peach juice and in and out of jeans. I'm objectifying every inch of her in my mind. TV has made me hate myself. Hate my bum, my breasts, because they don't look like canned fruit. It's not just on-screen nudity I need to be protected from, it's my own eyes, my own judgement. I've got good genes, I'm grateful it makes up for my lack of discipline – but I'm not made out of syrupy peaches. I'm made out of the hologram stretch marks where I grew so fast that summer, the faded evidence of chickenpox that I defiantly scratched as a kid, the changes in skin tone from sun cream applied liberally and then lazily on days at the beach that were too precious to spend caring. That's what being naked means. Bodies tell stories that peaches and cream can't. But they want nudity; nudity isn't nakedness, it would seem. Nudity is something else entirely.

I give my imaginary body double a made-up name – Wanda. I imagine the two of us on set, on the day of the nudity. I imagine her slipping the robe from her shoulders, carrying out her doubling par excellence – before looking at the camera straight down the lens.

Something clicks, her eyes shift. She stops, reels away from the camera and calls cut. I then imagine her stomping over to me, naked, lighting up a cigarette. She tries to pull the robe from my shoulders – renouncing body doubling everywhere! Demanding I be allowed to represent my own body, my own skin! She's had enough of selling lies! She pulls the robe from me and I'm suddenly naked, I see the entire cast and crew shield their eyes as though blinded by an apocalyptic light, as my nakedness is exposed by Wanda. She's yanking my robe, trying to torch it with her cigarette lighter! We pull the robe back and forth between us like two wild dogs with the same chew toy.

'Let them see you!' she cries, as she throws the flaming bathrobe like a Molotov cocktail into the studio.

'Hello? Hello? You still on the line?'

How many clauses did I just agree to?

'Yes, I'm still here.'

'I think it's a bad line. Did you hear the last part? We could word it so that you would have body-double *approval*.'

'I'd get to *choose* my body?'

'We could make that a priority.'

Wanda shakes her head at me, slow and menacing, smoke billowing heroically behind her.

'Do you know what? I'll sign wherever they want me to. If it calls for it, I'll do it. Just tell them I'll do it. All of it. Myself.'

INT. ACTRESS'S BEDROOM. MORNING.

ACTRESS *lies in bed, pink-heart duvet stuck to her face. The familiar half a glass of white wine on the chest of drawers. Salad from a kebab leads a trail to the scene of the crime.*

ACTRESS *talks in her sleep.*

> ACTRESS
> '... a vaccine to cure all of mankind ...'

Then suddenly the surprise of skin on skin, spine on spine. She jolts awake and turns.

RANDOM *sleepily turns to spoon her. ACTRESS uses all of her core strength to hold in a boozy fart. It's too much effort, she lets go.*

> RANDOM
> Hello?

> ACTRESS
> Hello?

                    RANDOM
        Yeah. Yeah? Hello?

                    ACTRESS
        Who — hello?

                    RANDOM
        Thanks for the sleepover.

                    ACTRESS
                 (*to herself*)
        So many blanks.

                    RANDOM
        Nice room. Posters.

                    ACTRESS
        Yup.

ACTRESS *reaches over, checks the time on
her phone. A reminder pops up, a little
red phone graphic.*

Notification: 330 voicemails.

                    ACTRESS
        Wow.

                      199

                    RANDOM
     You want to go again?

ACTRESS *turns*. RANDOM *has lifted the*
duvet, exposing himself to her. She
catches her breath, looks away.

                    ACTRESS
       It's late.

RANDOM *moves in for a morning kiss.*
ACTRESS *is frozen. He gets the corner*
of her mouth. He kisses her again,
breathing her in. His face works to her
shoulder.

                    RANDOM
     Your skin. I didn't dream it. It's
     incredible. Don't be shy. It's so
     hot. It's like caramel, like honey
     dripping straight from the comb.
     Your hair — I've always wanted to
     have sex with a woman like you.

                    ACTRESS
     A woman like me? I'm not an android.

RANDOM *grabs her arm.*

                    RANDOM
I thought actresses liked
compliments?

                    ACTRESS
Because I'm an actress I should
be complimented into fucking you?
Your breath smells like something
the Natural History Museum would be
interested in.

                    RANDOM
Ha! I know you're an actress, but you
couldn't fake last night.

                    ACTRESS
Stop saying the word 'actress'!

ACTRESS's hand finds the half-empty
wine glass. She throws the contents on
RANDOM and the glass to the ground. It
smashes.. Breathless, she picks up a
broken shard.

                              CUT TO:

Character: Janet (20s–30s but to pass for teens).
Breakdown: High school geek turned beauty queen. Taken under the wing of the popular crowd, a shy woman's high school experience is turned upside down, until her unexpected suicide.
Project: US/semi-autobiographical six-parter for cable.

Red carpet is a verb. I've lost two days waiting for some clothes to arrive. You always hear about actors being sent clothes for these things but this is the first time it's happened to me.

A huge black bag is finally delivered with the designer's name on it in shiny Braille on the side. It's tied with pale pink ribbon that smells like freshly cut grass. I slip my hand in, the clothes inside *feel* like money. It's really something when you're suddenly in close proximity to clothes you could *never* afford. The depth of the velvet on the sleeve of one of the jackets is addictive, I can't stop rubbing it. The beading on one of the handbags is so lively it looks like it's laughing. There's a peach satin dress that is so delicate it could be made from skin. I'm having a spontaneous fashion-gasm.

When the clothes don't fit, I sit naked on the bed and prod myself. If my thighs were the same diameter as my knees, it would be fine. Or if my shoulders were a little more like my ankles maybe. I cry like a spoiled brat. These clothes have spoiled me in the few minutes they've been in my care. The PR from the brand is very apologetic. She'll get them picked up straight away – but not replaced, I notice. I assumed they had my measurements. Or do *they* assume all women they dress are this size? Women with legs the size of kneecaps and backs the size of clenched fists.

The bag is collected how I imagine black-market kidneys are. A bearded courier in grey leathers turns up at my door unannounced. He disappears the bag into a messenger compartment on the back of his bike and gets me to sign with an 'X'. I imagine the bag bouncing against organs in iceboxes as he speeds away. I feel like a baby who's had its rattle taken. Indignant. Powerless. I should end my private shame here, watching the expensive clothes disappear down the road as I stand here in some Cookie Monster boxer briefs. The Cookie Monster eats a beloved cookie, it looks like he's just pulled it out of your arse, crumbs spray from his mouth as he exclaims – 'Cookie!'

I decide to call a friend. The friend who coined fashion-gasm. He knows about this kind of thing, this odd kind of heartbreak.

'Hey, what do you do when the clothes they loan you don't fit?'

You *don't* go in your briefs apparently. You invite a stranger into your personal world of angst to make some clothes decisions for you.

'A stylist, babes!'

Waiting to be buzzed in by the stylist is definitely reminiscent of being called to the Headmistress's office. I hated uniform and anyone who wanted to uphold the uniform was the enemy. I'd alter it any way I could and was happy to pay the price. This feels like siding with the enemy. Having someone tell me what to wear again? I should just wear Cookie Monster and be done. I feel a bit dizzy. Because I was so nervous I wouldn't fit into these clothes either, I've been improvising a juice fast, which involves me downing shop-bought smoothies with the nutritional value of a stick of gum. I drink a Diet Coke whenever I need a jump-start. Weak with hunger, I lean on the door and it falls open. I'm immediately transported into a bright and clean world of cloth. The stylist is so – fresh. She smells like freshly cut grass too, clearly fashion's signature scent. We *bisous-bisous* and I feel slightly less like a seal about to be clubbed.

'People were really excited to send stuff for you!'

'For *me*?'

'Sure! People are excited by you.'

I'm in shock.

I spy the endless rail of clothes and my dopamine shoots up.

'There were some people who said no this time. But when you look amazing this weekend, that will all change.'

Note to self – there's a group of people who know who you are and like you and there's another group who don't like you and would rather see you dead than in their clothes.

'Let's try on.'

We walk over to the rail, the sugar rush hits, and the velvet and beads start to seduce me again.

'Wow.'

'Yeah, I know, right?'

I tug on a brilliant-white dress with mesh sleeves that look like they're crafted from spiders' webs. It's a piece of art.

'I love this.'

'Oh, those rails are for my other clients. Sorry, babe. Here's you here.'

The smallest sliver of the rail is for *my* considera-tion. I thought people were excited to dress me? I pull out the first of four hangers, lift it to the light. Is this – cowhide? It could have been pulled from a Christmas panto.

'Really important piece, that would look great on you.'

I reach for the second hanger and swing it out to the light expectantly. A lace dress that I can see my hands through.

'Where's the dress that goes under this?'

'That one's all about strategic underwear.'

The dress is zipped up around my hungry body. It's the colour of setting plaster against my gold-tone skin, the stylist keeps calling it nude. I am nude, underneath this, I am nude and this nude on *my* nude looks like a nasty flare-up of psoriasis.

'With a nude heel? Fabulous.'

The 'nude' heel makes me look like I've just stepped into some vitiligo. The generalised 'nudeness' in this world is starting to feel as uncomfortable as the clothes.

'I might take another look.'

My hand finds some reassuring plain black satin.

'Can't wear black.'

'Oh?'

'First red carpet, can't wear black.'

'Can I try it?'

'I suppose you can. You could make it interesting with a nail. Or a shoe. Or a bag. But it's essentially boring and that designer doesn't dress anyone exciting. Ever.'

'Maybe I could slip it on, for comparison?'

The stylist looks like she wants to punch me as she zips me in. It looks lovely. Just lovely. It fits, simply. It's not trying to be anything other than what it is. Most important of all, my expression is relaxed, open. Happy.

'Yeah, it's not going to work.'

'Oh. I like it. I feel comfortable.'

'In the mirror.'

'Excuse me?'

'In the *mirror* you feel all those things. But in front of a camera lens, different story. It'll look so flat, I don't even think a lip would make it pop.'

The cameras – of course! But I can't wear the skin-graft dress, it might look great in the pictures but what about when I'm talking to *real* people? In *real* life? I'll be semi-naked psoriasis girl.

'What about *this* one?'

She holds up my final option. Another satin number. From far away it's simply cut like the black one, a rich shade of pearl. I move closer, run my hands over the fabric, and I'm suddenly hit by the smell of stale cigarette smoke. It has threads loose all over it, like it's been slept in. The back is pockmarked with hot rock burns! Some filthy toupee tape around the low-plunging neckline comes off on my hand. And is that – vomit? There's a cloudy orange stain with a watermark around it, a telltale odour.

'Trust me.'

She holds it up against me and it smells like I just woke up fully dressed after an orgy.

'OK.'

'It's all about the back. You can get lots of over-shoulder shots in this.'

Huge, colourful costume jewels bob free from their threads, like a cluster of gouged eyes.

'Is this what Amy Winehouse was wearing when she – died? I think I recognise it.'

'OK, so, what you need to know about posing for the cameras is this – the flash mattifies *everything*. This won't even show up.'

One of the loose gems makes a break for freedom, it's clearly fed up of the bullshit too, it rolls along the floor to an awkward stop.

'It came straight from a shoot in Milan, this happens all the time. If you hang it up while you have a shower, the steam will sort it. *Trust me.*'

Red Carpet Day arrives in a haze of Snickers and panic shopping. I have the 'I survived a nuclear disaster' dress and the racist nude heels, but my anxiety won't let me not get a backup option. A panic shop will help the panic.

The security at Selfridges mistake me for a member of staff, I get there so early. As soon as the doors open, I weave through the designer concessions, beads of panic perspiration forming on my top lip. I can buy a gown and bring it back tomorrow. I size up the coiffed, power-dressed sales representatives effortlessly trailing intense woody musks around me. I come to the conclusion that my fronting skills would not hold up if I was to bring something back to the store, sans tag, citing an imaginary faulty stitching excuse.

'Georgio does not stitch! He *binds*!' I imagine one of them shouting in my face before frogmarching me through the emergency exit. Maybe I could just buy one for real, a keepsake of my first red carpet experience. I walk over to the simplest gown on the least anorexic mannequin. The price tag looks like a GCSE maths equation. I leave via the food hall.

Back out on the high street, gourmet cupcake in hand, the countdown has begun. I pass the generic shops, but nothing looks like it will work 'on camera'. This idea that clothes that look nice in real life will suddenly disfigure me in front of camera lenses has me sweating from every orifice. I duck away down a side street known for interesting boutiques, maybe there's something vintage that could pass? I stop outside a tiny shopfront, a costume-hire shop. A costume is what I need! Something to hide inside. My hands are shaking. I drop the remainder of the cupcake which splays thick buttery icing all over the doorstep. Well, I have to go in now.

Inside, mannequins strike curious poses in clothes from another time. It's like being back in my dressing-up box as a child. Nothing matches and I'm suddenly at home. My eye is instantly drawn to the mannequin lounging in the highest spot in the room. I can see ruffles, I can see satin, I can see individuality. I can see me.

'Can I try that?' I hurriedly ask the sales assistant dressed as a sixties air stewardess.

'That's been up there for a long time. I don't think it's ever been tried before. It's vintage Givenchy.'

It's couture! It's costume and couture *and* for hire! I'm high from the butter icing.

'It would be so amazing if I could try it on. It's my first red carpet.'

The words 'red' and 'carpet' seem to work like 'open' and 'sesame'. There isn't enough the go-go-booted stewardess can do to help me now. She gets the ladder from the back. I steady it as she plucks the mannequin diva, in all of her reclining glory, out of her resting place. I take the legs, she has the rest. Dust bunnies rain down. Then one of her arms falls off. The legs come loose in my hand. We tear her apart as the assistant descends the ladder. The dress comes loose and falls to the ground as the mannequin woman lies naked and in pieces at our feet. She looks how I feel. The atmosphere is suddenly ominous.

The assistant picks up the dress, and starts to shake free the choking levels of dust.

'Do you know, if you hang it up in the bathroom while you have a shower the steam will sort it.'

Maniacal, camp laughter rings out across the shop. Who is that? As the saleswoman looks at me the way a paramedic might look at someone mid-stroke, it dawns on me. The laughter is mine.

I stand in front of my bedroom mirror and google 'red carpet posing'. Hundreds of sites have helpfully collated some of the most popular and successful ones for reference. I click on one. Models, actresses and pop stars, working their signature red carpet stance for the cameras. Their poses have all been given catchy signature titles with a step-by-step guide to achieving them so that normal people like me can live vicariously in front of the camera. There's the 'Cross Over', where a woman crosses one leg in front of the other to give the appearance of having very slim thighs. There's the 'Chin Scraper', where to show off a detail on the back of your dress, or just your very toned spine, you look over your shoulder with your chin attached to your shoulder. The trick to this one is the expression, it seems to be sold on looking as though you had turned your back for a moment when hordes of photographers suddenly appeared, your eyes widen and your mouth opens ever so coquettishly with surprise. There's the 'Teapot', which is one arm on your hip – the handle – with your shoulder up and back to create a thinner arm and décolletage. I scroll down frantically. There's the handle but where's the spout? Where's the bloody spout? There isn't one, thank God for that, the 'Teapot' is an interpretative name. Good. I think it suits me best. I strike the 'Teapot' as best as I can and take a photo in the vomit dress, send it to my fashion friend. He messages back immediately.

> What the fuck? What's all that stuff on it? Are you eating at the moment? You don't look well.

I look at the Givenchy on the bed. The shower trick actually worked, the era-spanning dust lifted right off. I slip it on. It fits. I take a picture and send.

> It's a risk, but at least you look like yourself. You're actually smiling. Why are you doing that with your arm?

I'd accidentally done a spout instead of a handle. I'm crashing.

The buzzer goes, the self-titled glam squad drag suitcases so heavy they look like there's more people inside them. They come through the door in a flurry of European kissing styles; the apartment fills with the scent of freshly cut grass. They spread a glamour buffet on my kitchen table in minutes. Do I have enough hair and face for all of that to go on?

'A nude would look good on you,' the immaculate human make-up woman chirps, already twiddling a lipstick offering from the table of sweetmeats.

'*No* nude! Sorry. Thank you. Anything else, just – never nude.'

'Do you want your hair to *say* something?' the equally immaculate hair man asks as he rubs my scalp, pulling my short hair in between his fingers.

'If it could say something, but not too loudly?'

An hour and a half later they put a mirror in front of me. My face is gleaming. Like I've been running but the sweat has only gone to the really flattering parts of my face. There are hollows in my cheeks that I've never seen. Long brown stripes up the sides of my jawline make me look like I was born with cheekbones. So *this* is how they do it! The false lashes remind me of Donald Duck's girlfriend Daisy who I always idolised. They'd drive Donald to distraction.

*

I put the stylist to the back of my mind as I clunk down to the car in the Givenchy. The men who work in the off-licence all stop and wave at me. I give a clipped royal wave before scooping the dress up ready to jump in. I stop in my tracks. The car is less 'let's go to the ball' and more 'let's go surfing'. It's a mud-flecked family car with a surfboard strapped to the top. The driver winds his window down.

'Be careful back there, we're just back from holiday.'

This is a mortal minicab not a superhuman Escalade. I duck in and balance on the edge of the seat, the only part free of dog hair.

'Let's get you there.'

The car lurches forward as my heels fill with sand.

You know you're near the carpet before you're even near the carpet.

Authorised personnel are given the rights usually saved for police. They direct the famous-people traffic one way and everyone else another. The queue of cars is long and glamorous, bar ours. The other cars have blacked-out windows, little statuettes. I have a *surfboard*. A tourist takes a photo. I'd feel humiliated if my Spanx weren't cutting off any human emotion. Suddenly, there are flashes of light like alien landings up ahead. There's no turning back. Then there it is, just like the pictures. The deep red velvet of the carpet. It's as well known as any person walking on it. It looks so soft. By now my heart is beating in my face. My lips are suddenly as dry as the desert in comparison to my forehead which is as oily as an avocado.

I thank the driver through gritted teeth. If he doesn't give any fucks about his battered vehicle driving along this carpet, then I shouldn't care that I look like I just finished grilling a cheese sandwich. I slam the door and smooth the front of my dress, something that I've only seen women do in films up until now. I smooth my dress, I smooth my hair, I adjust my bralette. It's the lingerie equivalent of a piece of cooked spaghetti, it's been thrown at my breasts and I'm hoping it will stick. I'm suddenly hit by the reality that I don't have a coat on and it's February. I'm so freezing my chest starts to vibrate. Doesn't matter. Think of the finish line. This is a computer game. Stepping out of that car and onto the carpet gets you points. Walking like a human being inside of your dress is points. Subtly pulling down your slimming undergarments without the cameras seeing – points. Waving to fans behind the barriers like you're a Hollywood star and making them *think* they recognise you, bonus points plus infinity lives.

My ears try to tune out the constant screams of the crowd. There are famous people everywhere. There's a Hollywood actress I have loved since I was a *child*, literally paces away from me. I could run and hug her, and it wouldn't even be a run, it would be a shuffle. She's a *shuffle* away! She looks so – *shiny*. We're all so shiny on this side of the barriers. My eyes adjust and I can

suddenly see how thin she is. Looking at her baby dino-
saur spine through her backless dress makes me suck
cold air through my teeth. How is she so luminous?
Where the hell is it coming from? How do you power a
body that small? From the other side of the barriers, on
the other side of the TV cameras, I bet she looks how she
always looks – normal. But I'm here now, a shuffle away,
and I can see the layer of soft downy hair on her arms
and face, covered expertly by the now-familiar iridescent make-up. There were girls at school who stopped
eating and had that hair. They'd hide long sideburns
under headbands. I remember a girl a couple of years
above us who had it all over her back. She nearly died.

I avert my eyes and literally bump into a European
heartthrob at the top of the carpet. I'm in the early stages
of hypothermia and my bones are shaking. I've got little
to no coordination left. He's turned round and arrested
me with those dark, expressive eyes I know so well
from his films. I've stood on him and he doesn't seem to
mind. He's asking if I'm OK. My hearing is underwater
because of the screams and the shivering.

'I'm OK! Good luck tonight!'

I'm shouting in his face. Oh my God, I *love* him.
He's an incredible actor. So beautiful. He's talking to me
again – he wants me. Oh. No. Someone next to him is
talking to me. His assistant is asking if I want his big
awards umbrella. It's started to snow and I didn't feel it.
My hair is wet, my eyelashes are wet, my bralette is losing its stick. Minus ten points! The assistant is looking at

me like a kindly doctor before they tell you it's terminal . I had better take the umbrella. I thank her. She's enviably fully clothed, fur-lined boots and a parka. I reach out and tap the wonderful actor on the arm – the hypothermia has spread to my brain now and I feel a strong need to tell him how brilliant he is. Maybe let him know the fertile days in my cycle. He turns round with such a look of disdain that I lose my footing again. I pretend I was helping wipe some snow off his arm. He doesn't thank me. Mostly because he didn't have snow on his arm. The paparazzi are calling his name and he walks boldly out into the glare of the most flashbulbs I've ever seen. It's like he's the Taj Mahal. Every time the European actor smiles or waves for them, they blind me.

'Step this way.'

A lady with a clipboard and an earpiece is putting gentle pressure on my arm. She's nodding towards the flashbulbs. I don't think I have enough points to go to the next level. Maybe I can just stay here, become a snowflake. But I'm walking. She's holding the umbrella and I'm walking. Where am I walking? I stop roughly in the middle of an enormous bit of red carpet. It was long and straight and now it's spilled out of itself like a tongue. A couple of the photographers know my name and yell it *really loud*.

The cameras start. No, I was just … walking to the spot, I wasn't posing, I was just walking to the place. I look at clipboard lady for moral support. She gestures to a small X stuck to the carpet. Try to remember the poses. Thin arms on hips, teapot no spout, thin legs. I can feel my hands vaguely on my hips. It's only supposed to be one. The cameras flash.

'Over here, over here, over here, over here!'

I have no sensation in my body. Before losing consciousness completely, another woman with a clipboard moves towards me in slow motion. Is it over now? For some reason, I wave at the photographers. I'm so relieved, my arm shoots up and waves. I don't even have the energy to regret it. I lean into the woman with the clipboard, put all my weight on her like she's escorting me from a moon mission, my legs adjusting to gravity.

Level complete. Inside. Mini bottle of champagne comes past on a tray. Bonus points. I take my bag that looks like it once belonged to one of the Borrowers it's so small, slide my phone out and text 'Never again.' Send.

There's a genuine moment of happiness at the post-awards meal when I realise I'll be the only one eating bread. I finish a whole basket of artisanal rolls. My face thaws. Outside, unofficial paparazzi collect like mucus around the mouth of the back exit. They yell violent words, try to get a rise out of actresses, skid into the gutter to try and get shots up their skirts. The bulbs stop when I appear. Fine by me.

When a black cab pulls up with his light on, I feel like crying. I didn't want to get cold again.

'You look nice,' says the cabbie.

'Thanks. So do you.'

'Ayyyyy! Won't tell the wife.'
'Can we stop at an off-licence on the way?'

I make my duvet into a tent, balance my glass on the mattress. Google my name plus 'red carpet', hit the return key. A world of darkness opens up in the half-light. There are already pictures of me online. Blogs dedicated to red carpet shame light up like Christmas trees.

Spacetobreathe at 21:07

Ill-fitted, boring, uninspired, poor styling. It's a NO.
All over the place.

Jolie_files at 22:50

She looks like my learning disabled nephew.

MaryKateandAshleyUnofficial at 22:55

'All over the place.'
Well said.

Swinton95 at 22:56

She's got it so wrong. Her posture is appalling and is it
just me or are one of her boobs lower than the other?
Her boobs are wonky. Her eyebrows look like she drew
them in with an off-center stencil and a sharpie.

Leonardoismylove at 23:01

When you have short hair you have to be SO sure.

Another alert, my phone this time. I balance the
wine on the keyboard. Stylist Mob has sent a text.

What happened? X

INT. GENERIC PUBLICITY OFFICE,
SOHO. DAY.

ACTRESS *sits on a very low chair
in a hipster office. She constantly
struggles to find a comfortable position.*
JOURNALIST *checks the recorder on her
iPhone is still running.*

> JOURNALIST
> So, what does it feel like to be
> having a breakout moment?

> ACTRESS
> Does this chair seem low to you?

> JOURNALIST
> I'm OK. You're taller than me though.

> ACTRESS
> I feel like Alice in fucking
> Wonderland.

JOURNALIST *laughs.* ACTRESS *doesn't. The*
JOURNALIST *makes a note.*

> ACTRESS
> What was the question, sorry?

                    JOURNALIST
What does it feel like to be having a
breakout moment?

                      ACTRESS
When I think of a breakout, I think
of my chin a few days before my
period. Or Free Willy jumping over
the sea wall.

                    JOURNALIST
Five-star reviews, iconic
performances. You're riding a wave.

                      ACTRESS
Now I feel like I've successfully
completed a spate of crimes.

JOURNALIST *scribbles more notes.* ACTRESS
tries harder.

                      ACTRESS
I was just being — never mind.

JOURNALIST *smiles and shrugs, checks her*
phone is recording.

                    ACTRESS
It's — *wonderful* — to be riding a
wave, as you say. I mean, I've
been acting for a long time. So,
I suppose the saying is true —
it takes a lifetime to become a
newcomer.

                    JOURNALIST
Exactly. How does it feel to be doing
awards and red carpet?

                    ACTRESS
How does it FEEL?

                    JOURNALIST
Exactly.

                    ACTRESS
I wouldn't say it feels like any—

                    JOURNALIST
Who do you like to wear?

                    ACTRESS
Who rather than what?

JOURNALIST *makes more notes on the pad.*

                    ACTRESS
This is all being recorded, why do
you need the — pad?

                    JOURNALIST
Just so I don't forget details.

ACTRESS *writhes in the chair.*

                    JOURNALIST
You play an amazing character
in your show.

                    ACTRESS
Thank you.

                    JOURNALIST
So strong, and quirky and interesting.
Something totally different.

                    ACTRESS
Really? Well, thank you.

                    JOURNALIST
Exactly. Does it have an impact on
who you're dating?

                    ACTRESS
I'm sorry?

JOURNALIST
Does it have an impact on your love
life? Who are you dating right now?

ACTRESS
Are you asking if playing strong women
has an adverse impact on my love life?

JOURNALIST
If you're dating another actor I
guess they understand.

ACTRESS
You're asking if I'm fucking someone
famous?

JOURNALIST
Sorry?

ACTRESS
You want to know what I wear and
if you might have heard of who I'm
sleeping with? Is that it?

ACTRESS *laughs*.

JOURNALIST
I really love your work, that's not
what I'm asking.

ACTRESS *takes a sip of water from the cup on the table.*

                    ACTRESS
          Sorry, I'm tired.

                    JOURNALIST
          I can start over with another
          question.

                    ACTRESS
               (*rubbing her temples*)
          Sure.

                    JOURNALIST
          What's your background?

                    ACTRESS
          As an actress?

                    JOURNALIST
          As — you. Your background, like where
          are you from?

                    ACTRESS
          I'm from Hackney.

                    JOURNALIST
                  (*nervous giggle*)
        No, sorry, where are you *actually*
        from?

Pause.

                     ACTRESS
        Hackney. I grew up in Hackney. I'm
        from London.

                    JOURNALIST
                 (*giggles again*)
        Sorry, I mean, sorry, I mean — where
        are you *really* from?

ACTRESS *is silent.*

                    JOURNALIST
        OK, a sore spot.

She scribbles.

                     ACTRESS
        Did you just write 'attitude'?

                                    CUT TO:

```
Character: Nina, ageless.
Breakdown: Tragic heroine. An actress
spirals into substance abuse when her
contract with the studio ends.
Project: TV movie.
Notes from casting: Think Marilyn, but
ethnic.
```

'What the hell am I doing drinking in L.A. at twenty-six?'
The question repeated over and over in the chorus of
'Drinking in L.A.' from the one-hit-wonder rockers,
Bran Van 3000. In Los Angeles for the first time, I catch
myself singing it under my breath almost constantly.
When I hear it play in bars or cabs or out of a portable
speaker strapped to a hipster's pushbike, it feels like being winked at. I wink back. Apparently it's 'a good time
to be here' because of the work I'm doing. You have to
'feed the heat', an expression everyone seems to use at
any opportunity.

I stay with an old acquaintance from drama school.
She's kind and bright, has always been talented and
beautiful. But the girl I meet in Los Angeles is quite
changed. I get a ride from the airport, and when I find
her at her studio apartment in a neighbourhood I recognise from nearly every American film I've ever watched
ever, she hugs me and I can feel bone. Within minutes of
dumping my bag on the single bed she's lovingly made
up for me, she's updated me on her existence here; it's

a lifetime away from life back home. She works nights as a waitress – which again makes her sound like some of my favourite characters ever from American movies. Her eyes lower and she suddenly stops mid-sentence.

'I totally forgot I have to Skype with my love guru!'

And it's touchdown in LA. I swallow my English cynicism and tell her I'm fine to take a long walk round the neighbourhood. She explains that the guru is to help her find true love in alternative ways. The guru seems to charge through the nose for his personalised 'love cleanse'. The package includes a tailor-made diet of raw green vegetables, which I see looming in the studio kitchenette, and a list of dos and don'ts for interpersonal interactions. No unnecessary touching is a big part of what he endorses. No sex either.

'I wasn't actually supposed to hug you just then.'

'Don't worry, I didn't inhale.'

It's a joke that doesn't mean anything. She doesn't laugh even out of politeness. I can feel my British irony haemorrhaging. The love guru also suggests, of course, that she makes dream boards to give maximum strength to her cosmic ordering. This is basically a mental ordering-in service, a Deliveroo from your brain to the universe. The dream boards are huge pieces of card that adorn every inch of free wall space. They're emblazoned with glittery aspirational quotes and pictures cut from magazines. Cut-outs of what she wants. Smiling women in bikinis with their ribs showing, the logos of popular US television networks, award-winning actresses feigning modesty as they clutch gold statuettes, their knuckles white. There's one board that only has green foods that are hard to eat on it. Kale, when cut out and put on a piece of cardboard with a colourful felt-tip outline, is surprisingly aspirational-looking. I ask if her guru is on holiday, hence the Skype.

'No, we only Skype. That's his thing.'

'Doesn't want to get too close to people, huh?'

'Maybe.'

'So, you've only seen this guy from the waist up?'

She doesn't understand. I'm through the looking glass in a world where carbohydrates and innuendo are not welcome. I swallow my retorts.

'How long have you been paying him?'

'We've been *spiritually connected* for about a year now.'

'Cool. Have you found love?'

'It's more about the journey of loving yourself.'

'Sure, of course, but – you want a boyfriend at some point? A girlfriend?'

'I'm not there yet. Another year and I might be.'

A whole year of getting paid to tell people they need to eat vegetables and not touch people? I need to change my vocation!

'Well, say hi from me.'

I take a lap of the block.

*

I wake up out of jet lag to the sound of a woman's voice. Soft, deliberate. The husky Californian tones of a woman who sounds stoned out of her tree.

'You're a strong, confident woman,' she tells me. 'Awaken your inner goddess.'

I would if I wasn't so jet-lagged. I sit up in bed and take a look across the studio. The voice isn't speaking to me, it's coming from the bathroom.

'I am a goddess,' an English voice answers back.

My friend comes out of the bathroom, fresh from the shower. She looks suddenly sheepish.

'Did I wake you?'

'No. No. Do those things work?'

'Mantras?'

'Yeah.'

'They're part of my spiritual growth.'

I can't argue with that.

'It's a series.'

'From the guru?'

'I'm going to hot yoga.'

'Really? I'll come.'

When in Rome! I'm someone who has to be cajoled into exercise, scared into it with photos of decaying limbs and fat-clogged arteries, like on a cigarette packet. I have a sports bra handy, an aspirational bit of packing, but nothing else. She lends me some leggings from her 'before' drawer. Before LA. Before the cleanse. These are the only ones I'll fit into, clearly. The ones from the 'after' drawer look like I'd have to wear them more as a scarf.

She drives us. A CD of more incantations starts with the engine. She switches to FM radio.

The yoga class is hot and *hot*. I don't know when I've seen this many good-looking people all glowing, all sweating, all in close proximity. I graduate from admirer to pervert in about three yoga positions. I'm turned on and totally intimidated. These people flow like water, they are slim yet powerful, all of them, they slide in and out of positions while I'm working every part of my mid-section just to stop myself from farting. In a particularly humiliating pose, my eyes drift to the raised leg of a woman at the front of class. I notice her because she's twinkling, like a fairy trapped in the full-length mirrors. There are windows in the ceiling and the rays are making her skin sparkle. I wipe the sweat from my eyes and crane my neck. I see clearly now that it's because she's wearing a gold bikini. The fabric is almost blindingly glittery as she rolls onto her side. I wonder if I'm the only one who can see her because she looks more like an apparition than an actual person doing exercise. Are the toxins leaving my body making me hallucinate? She's not sweating. She has a light gold body halo. She's my Hollywood golden statuette. My reason for being here. She lifts her leg out to the side, and her panties don't move. Her golden panties stay in place. There's sweat pouring from everywhere on every other body in here, my freckles are sliding off me it's so hot. But the gold lamé on her butt stays in freeze-dried position. The tiny triangles over her nipples don't expose any-thing other than two perfectly proportioned mounds of breast. These are the types of vision that come to you when you're about to have a cardiac arrest. That and smelling burnt toast, right? I take a deep breath in – *can* I smell burning? Head rush. I haven't actual-ly been breathing this entire class. No burning toast but she is still there. I can make out the soft glow of her effortless body. Every time she flows, she emits a visible heatwave, like a hot Cadillac bonnet in the desert of an eighties music video. She is breathing and flowing and that gold lamé is as secure as two vacuum-packed chicken nuggets. Jealousy is where love and hate meet, right? I love her and I hate my-self. It's not about body comparison or being good at yoga, it's her lack of self-consciousness. She looks like she isn't plagued by a damn thing. Her bikini stays in place not because she wills it to, but because she *expects* it to. There is a blissful absence of self-doubt that glows as intensely as the deep gold of her swimwear. I don't think it's an expression I've ever seen on myself. We look strangely similar I realise, a likeness that might see us side by side in a police line-up but maybe not quite mistaken for sisters. The teacher calls the class to an end and asks us to shut our eyes for silent meditation. It's over? Have I been moving at all? I must have been. I feel physically broken and exalted and horny. I keep my eyes open until the last moment to admire my apparition's whole body, stretched out, lying back like a dangerous mermaid on a rock, an easy dip in her middle back that doesn't even look like it spells early lower-lumbar issues. She's still smiling. She's enjoying herself immensely, deriving so much pleasure from the simple act of lying still on the floor. She doesn't fiddle or play with her bikini at all. It's still dutifully yielding to her flesh. I close my eyes. The sun is beginning to really beat down and the insides of my eyelids go that red colour where you can see your blood and your veins. Magically these tiny thread veins start to sparkle. Little luminous clusters just twinkle there. A constellation of bright planets and star formations swirl and glint and burn away. Am I being absolved? Will a lifetime of overthinking, of cultural cynicism, now somehow go away? Will I skip carefree along LA freeways hitching rides to a new me? My friend taps me on the arm. The room is empty. End of class. I'm like a big dog woken from a dream, I kick my legs ungracefully and flip over sideways. She's gone. My statuette. She's gone.

'Scuse me for a sec.'

I power-walk out to the reception area, through to the changing rooms, poke my head into the toilets. It's like she was never there. I'm perspiring at double the rate I was doing the actual yoga.

'You OK?'

'Yeah, just thought I saw someone I knew.'

We don't even see her in the communal shower area. Would I recognise her without the bikini? Again, like a big dumb dog, I hang my head out of the car window as we reverse out of the parking lot, tongue lolling, panting to see her again. I can't imagine her wearing normal clothes.

'How did you find the class?'

'Good, it was good. Tough. Can we come again tomorrow?'

'That particular class isn't on again until next week. You might want a break before you do it again?'

She's right, I look like an ambulance may need to be called.

'Let's book ahead. I like to keep in shape.'

The next few days are filled with meetings. Meetings in huge buildings with extraordinary views and security tighter than airports. Meetings in hotel lobbies for carbonated water and lemon. Meetings in brasseries for smoothies. Meetings on verandas for non-coffee-coffee and non-pastry-pastries, and always on the company card.

The buzzwords that start out as seductive – 'exciting', '*heat*', 'fresh' – are eventually exhausting. There seems to be a language that powerful people use out here to say everything and nothing all at once. To talk about the present in a way that makes your future seem certain but without committing to you at all. You feel a million dollars and fifty cents at the same time. It reminds me of the first time I tried candyfloss, those huge puffs of pink sugar looked like you'd be full for days but dissolved instantly into sweet nothing in your mouth. My own words dissolve around my teeth. When I speak I don't recognise my own voice, I sound like a bad actor reciting a bad script. The script doesn't improve with any of the calls to my agent back home.

'They can't sell you right now – they'll keep you in the mix.'

Can't sell me? They said they loved me! L.O.V.E. That's not a can-do Californian attitude, that's split-personality syndrome! Keep me in the mix? I'm not an egg! How could they say they want me and not want me? I could never do that. The British way is sticking to your word even if it gives you a stress-related ulcer. This is the steadiest stream of rejection I've experienced in my career. This is terrible for an over-thinker. An over-thinker with jet lag. I'm the common denominator in these stalled relationships. I think they could tell I was an over-thinker 'in the room'. They could tell I wasn't going to be able to *do* Hollywood. That my brain won't switch off when required. Come to think of it, perhaps when they asked me what kinds of roles I thought I could be playing, I should have avoided naming male French actors from the sixties. That doesn't say 'Cast me!' One of the agents called me 'pretty and funny', or was it just – 'pretty funny'?

Either way I should have smiled and said 'Bless you, darling,' not 'I've always wanted to play a serial killer.' I may have even joked about not going to the gym – I mean, it's not a joke, but it may have given them wind of my reluctance towards nudity or even just tight-fitting clothing. Have I not learned a thing from the movies I grew up watching? Actor goes for a meeting in a skyscraper, their moth-eaten overcoat the only thing of value they have in the world, the agent asks how far they're willing to go, they say, 'All the way,' they shake hands and they sign. The film cuts to the actor swimming lengths outside his mansion. What I *need* to be, what I *should* have been, is the woman in the gold bikini. Effortlessly shimmering, beguiling and untouchable with a constant hint of a smile. No complex thoughts, no self-searching or self-deprecation, no need to buck a trend in this town, just gold water spilling into the glass of anyone who wants to drink. I need to get back to yoga class. I need to see her again, study her movements, engage her in conversation if I can. Learn her ways, wipe my brow clear of thoughtful frowning, smooth it with iridescent apathy.

Sunk in a leatherette couch of another over-air-conditioned reception, the same successful faces stare up at me from the magazines. I lean sideways, their eyes follow. I stare back, start to practise the ethereal smile of the girl in the gold bikini. I let my lips curl up to the sides, but not too much. The corners of my mouth won't stop juddering. Relax. I smooth out the frown lines in my forehead, lift my eyebrows in that way that makes it feel like you've had a facelift, an expression of mild surprise or passing wind. That feels about right. I let the smile appear a little more on my lips, the forehead feels so right I'm sure I can afford that little extra upturn of the corners of the mouth. No, it's too much. This expression is so specialised! The smallest attempt to personalise it throws it wildly out of whack, instead of aloof I suddenly look like one of the serial killers I'm always looking for an opportunity to play. I physically rub the expression from my face, shake my cheeks, let my lips sag like an old helium balloon. I open my eyes and at my feet is a dog, a tiny Jack Russell staring up at me. Panting.

'That's Willy, he's the office dog. Say hi, Willy!' the receptionist chirps from her perch.

Once again I am gulping down a dry British retort. I scratch his ear.

'Hey, Willy.'

Willy takes that as a cue to jump on my lap.

'He likes you!'

The receptionist claps. At least someone in this town does.

'He's cute.'

I pet him, his head and his tummy, glad for the distraction. Willy makes himself comfortable. He lies on his back, his head on the leatherette and the rest of him on my lap. He then spreads his legs, wide for a small dog, and starts licking his balls. He doesn't stop. He keeps going until Willy's very tiny willy appears. I look over to the receptionist who's now suddenly very absorbed in urgent documents. He keeps going. He's getting right in there. He keeps looking up at me for approval, before diving back down. I laugh. I laugh a really real laugh. The first since I've been here. His little name tag jiggles, a bone with 'Willy' engraved on it with love. A British snort escapes. A smartly dressed man and woman walk in and the receptionist announces them as the agents I'm here to meet. I stop giggling and Willy free-rolls down my legs. He lands on his feet. No sign of a boner. He yawns. What a pro.

In the meeting room, I'm stuck with my own face. I haven't had time to practise the carefree smile. All I can think about is Willy's sexual abandon.

'That dog in the lobby is so cute.'

'He is, right?'

'He jumped on my lap and started licking his balls.'

There's a silence. I fill it.

'He wouldn't stop. It was frenzied. After ten days here, I think I know how he feels.'

The girl in the gold bikini appears on a broomstick in my mind, writing 'Death' across the sky, throwing her head back and cackling like a witch. The broomstick is Willy's penis. But then, the cackle becomes real laughter.

Warm and welcoming. It's coming from the man and woman in front of me.

'Well, that's the most memorable introduction *we've* had today.'

Back at home, my friend asks me how it went.

'They said they liked my work and admired my honesty. My humour. They were telling the truth, I think. Kale smoothie to celebrate?'

I think I see the girl in the gold bikini that night at a pool party, but it's a woman in a *silver* bikini, the light caught her for a moment and it dazzled gold. I finally open up to my friend and kind hostess as she drives me to the airport the following morning, her mantras playing softly as we speed along the highway. I am a *strong, confident woman.*

'Do you remember that woman in the gold bikini in yoga class that first day? I mean, *who* wears a bikini to yoga, right? Not standard by any means! Do you remember her?'

'Really? I don't remember a woman in a gold bikini.'

'What? She was right in front of us.'

'I've never seen a woman in a gold bikini! That would be a standout for sure, even for LA. That class is pretty serious about yoga.'

'Will you look again? When you go again next week? Email me if she's there? Just for – fun, I guess.'

'Um ... sure, I'll take a look.'

'How's the love cleanse going anyway?'

'Oh, I'm done.'

'Really?'

'Yeah. I don't know if that love guru was for real.'

'Huh.'

I stare out of the passenger window.

INT. ACTRESS'S BEDROOM. DAY.

ACTRESS *stands, hands on hips, in an ill-fitting bra and pants. Her chest rises and falls. She wipes beads of sweat from her stomach.*

Her laptop balances precariously on the duvet. A blonde Californian woman chirps away, free from sweat, through some leg lifts.

ACTRESS *tries, sporadically, to keep up. Every time she gets into a rhythm, the woman falls into a new routine — followed effortlessly by the other women in the background of the video.*

ACTRESS *puts her head in her hands. 'This is as hard as it gets, come on!' the Californian woman's voice calls out against the synthesised pop.*

ACTRESS *suddenly starts some aggressive star jumps, erratic and out of sync with the video. Her lampshade falls to the ground.*

*The phone rings. 'Unknown number' flashes
on the screen.*

*She goes to the window, pulls the
curtain back, answers.*

> ACTRESS
>
> Are you here?

> AGENT
>
> It's me!

> ACTRESS
>
> Me?

> AGENT
>
> Me!

> ACTRESS
>
> Me?

> AGENT
>
> Your agent. Hello!

> ACTRESS
>
> I thought you were my pizza.

> AGENT
>
> Hahaha! No, unfortunately not!

                    ACTRESS
Your number didn't show —?

                     AGENT
I'm in LA, maybe that's why. Early
for a pizza?

                    ACTRESS
I've got — people — over.

The Californian woman on the screen
punches the air with pink weights -
'Come on, is that all you got?!'

                     AGENT
Ah! OK, I won't take up too much of
your time. Just wanted to check in,
see how you are.

                    ACTRESS
I'm really great. How are you?

                     AGENT
I'm so good, I feel so cleansed and
positive here, I love it. And they
love you! Your name is in all the
right circles. I think we should be
looking for some press opportunities
for you. Some events, some nice

press, keep your profile up. You know
what it's like out here, all about
the Starmeter.

ACTRESS

Starmeter?

AGENT

You know, your online ranking! Didn't
you talk about it when you were here?
It's a little meter that goes up or
down on the leading movie databases
depending on your profile.

ACTRESS

And mine's low on stars, is it?

AGENT

Haha! No! It's only down three
hundred and sixty-five this week.

ACTRESS

From what? Three hundred and sixty-
five?

AGENT

No! But wouldn't hurt to have your
face out there a little more? There's
been a couple of requests in for you.

                    ACTRESS
There have?

                      AGENT
Some pictures, some interviews, some
fashion stuff. I'll email you the
details.

                    ACTRESS
I'm not sure if —

The blonde Californian woman is
screaming again —'And that's your WORK
IT WORKOUT! I'm so proud of you.' The
sound of the women clapping themselves.

                      AGENT
Who was that?

                    ACTRESS
My friends.

                                CUT TO:

Character: Harriet, 30s—50s.
Breakdown: An escaped slave.
Project: Drama/historical/feature.
Notes from casting: Great role for a minority actress.

Clashing creatively with a director at work, I offer up an after-hours drink to clear the air. Her only gear for the past month has been to dismiss my ideas outright in the rehearsal room, and when she can't dismiss the ideas, she cuts my lines. I watch my colleagues start to hide behind their fingers every time I take centre stage. Over four weeks, the temperature inside my face has become so hot, it threatens to weld my lips together. I won't get the few words I have out if it goes on like this.

When your comrades can't quite look you in the eye over a boiling kettle at break time, it means the director – the head of the family – has chosen one child to pick on and it's you. There's often one member of the cast who gets targeted in this way. This time it's my turn.

When I suggest the drink, she's surprised. Eyes wide, she mentally scrolls through a calendar of non-existent plans and can't make one up quickly enough before I suggest we go now. She reminds me of how tall I am before accepting.

'You really are tall, aren't you? OK, fine, let's go for a drink. If that's what you want.'

'I'd love to talk something through.'

We sit down. Her drink is on me.

She takes a sip.

'I find you aggressive.'

I was poised to sip, settle in, dance around the subject of her passive assaults on my self-esteem before probably backing out of asking her for any kind of explanation at all. I mean, the belittlement is so deeply internalised now, why scratch at it? Whatever it is, it's probably my fault. I probably said something, did something without realising, and she's carrying a grudge and taking it out on me because of the stress of rehearsing difficult material.

Aggressive? Does she mean – tall? Because … I can't change that.

Instead of a polite dance, the bottom drops out of my stomach. Out of my world. No, the bottom drops out of my planet. The planet of me. The planet that has always tried to spin as closely to friendly planets and as far from aggro ones as possible. I've never been called aggressive out loud, but it's definitely something that's floated in the air. In expensive shops with shop assistants on guard against my walking in, at school with other parents telling teachers it's not fair when I win at sports, when maître d's of empty restaurants don't want to give me a table in case I – scare the chairs? Or when girls barge me on the dance floor to stop me from terrifying the locals with my freedom of movement. It's because the general cloud of my presence causes disruption that I want to orbit the chill planets, the ones with the spaceship landings, the ones little kids look up at through their telescopes and think … wow … that looks like a friendly planet – I sure hope when the epic floods hit, me and my family can afford a ticket up there. The planets where spring water is found, where snow suddenly falls freakishly and unprecedentedly and – most of all – softly on its previously thought inhabitable surface. The planets scientists like. That cartoonists personify with cute, dopey faces. I don't want to be with the planets that burn up, combust, unexpectedly go retrograde, causing celebrities to die suddenly and chaos to reign on planet Earth. I work unpaid overtime at not wanting people to think I mean them harm. So now the bottom falls out of everything I live on.

I feel myself falling slow-motion backwards in my chair and through an unknown universe. Breathing is shallow as I try and speak without an oxygen tank in a suddenly airless galaxy.

' … Aggressive?'

'I just find you aggressive.'

' … In what way?'

'I don't know. In every way. I just feel it.'

Options for how to react suddenly flash neon in my brain. A depraved game show starts up in my head. Do I:

(A) Go for being visibly all the shades of aghast?

(B) Apologise for my presence?

(C) Pretend I didn't hear the last part?

'Sorry, I didn't hear that last part?'

'I find you aggressive and that's it.'

'That's why you kept cutting my scenes? Why you won't incorporate my ideas? Ever?'

'There you go again. I wasn't "cutting your scenes". Your work just isn't as good as some of the others. OK?'

The flashing lights in my brain dim for an ad break and a desert wind starts to blow loud in my ears.

So many things to say.

Too many things to say.

Should say. Because there's now a queue of ancestors, blown up on that desert wind, standing behind me right now. The ancestors who fought for all the rights to be polite and all the rights to be rude – the rights to be. For me. I can see their battle scars clear, they're so close. They are risen and standing all around me. They're awake because their hard work is under threat of being harmed, erased a little bit. Their voices, if I don't speak, can't be heard. This woman has made assumptions about me. I'm locked in an assumption and my ancestors have come to get me out. To save my planet, so fiercely and delicately tended all these years by me. So painstakingly steered through the 'approachable woman of colour' constellation.

'OK …?'

'It was nothing – specific. Just a feeling.'

Oh, she's stuck on a feeling? A general feeling of aggression that filled up the room from my direction, all coming from my direction. Escape routes now start to flash in neon lights, part two of the game show of systemic cultural bias.

Option (A) flashes green: Tell her to go FUCK herself.

The ancestors, still at my back, shake their heads.

'That will prove her right!' they cry.

Yes. The foremothers have a point. Is it troubling that the choral voices of my beloved and most wise ancestors have been programmed into my brain as Simba's mum from *The Lion King*? Of course it is, but I don't have time to ponder internalised racism right now. I have to work out what to do.

'She wants you to react!' cries another voice.

Yes, of course, the best way to make someone who isn't in any way aggressive, aggressive, is to call them aggressive!

Option (B) flashes neon orange in my head: Pretend not to hear. Sudden and selective deafness is often my preferred route to conflict resolution.

Option (C) is a pleasing neon pink: Start to cry. Even though playing the victim when you know someone is trying to victimise you makes vomit rise in my throat, this strikes me as an option to please me and the ancestors. It's a game-show winner, surely.

'Speak your truth!' The ancestors are calling more loudly now.

I stare back at this woman, a woman swaddled so tightly in the cloth of her own aggression towards me that her eyes are visibly bulging.

'Only truth can conquer fear!' a voice from the back of the ancestral throng cries.

Option (D) flashes in a reassuring neon purple: Speak your truth. The ancestors close their eyes and smile. The gaudiness of the game show and the warm glow of the desert merge into a blanket of soft light. Option (D) it is then. My lips part and my heart opens.

'I've done my absolute best, for months, to collaborate with you. To work as a team. You've had a barrier up and I haven't been able to work out why, and that's only hinting partially at the pain it's caused me. I find *you* very aggressive.'

She goes for one of my earlier options – all shades of aghast.

She looks at me like the idea that she could be the aggressor is impossible. That is not an option, any option.

'This is your problem, not mine.'

She's now looking at me like the no sips of wine I've had might have made me drunk or delirious. Like she might go through my bag for drugs.

That word, that word 'aggressive' that just tumbled from her mouth with ease, belongs to me. The finger-pointing only goes one way – my way. That word only works to describe *me*. To build a picture of *me*. To build a safe arc to carry her words, her feelings, her fear across the stormy sea of *me*. My panic and my embarrassment, my shrunkenness and my self-doubt are the safe harbour she chooses to dock in.

Speaking the truth, even in these little bits, is pushing tears up to my eyes.

The ancestors are making noises, trying to get through the time barrier with their broken voices. I hear the splintering of sacred staffs, the smashing of lucky skulls, the fizzing of lightning and the rumble of tropical thunder. I hear the sound of night-time crickets, I hear the deafening wailing of entire tribes, the sound of babies crying. The sound of generations lifting up their voices – their deepest magic – to be heard. Or not to be heard so much as not to be silenced. None of this really fits in a west London sports bar. It threatens to throw our glasses off the table, damn near bring the walls in.

'Look, it's fine, not everyone sees eye to eye.'

'I'm really upset. What you've said. What you've just said has really upset me. Shaken me.'

The overwhelming vibrations of a mythical rattlesnake. The tears flow.

'Oh my gosh, this is such a surprise, I'm so sorry.'

She's surprised. She's surprised to see me vulnerable. It's not a possibility she's considered. That words based on assumptions might break me. That those simple words might unleash an ocean made up of the little sips of sadness that come from being repeatedly misinterpreted at a glance. My ability to be fragile is beyond her. All she sees is an aggressor. Someone she needs to protect herself from at all costs, protect an audience from. She's cutting me down on paper because she's scared not just for herself, but for everyone. The others who might have to witness me. She needs to spare them her discomfort. She clearly feels an audience would be happy for her to speak on their behalf. She's clinging to my aggression to keep other people safe. Safe from me and my posse of ancestors. If we shine, she might only glimmer. That. Is. Not. An option.

'All I've wanted is to feel like part of the group,' I say quietly.

'You are, you are, if only I'd known how much this was affecting you –'

Then what?

Then *what*?

'This has all been one big misunderstanding. Poor thing. You've taken this the wrong way.'

The ancestors are deathly quiet now, but I feel them there.

'Let's sweep this under the carpet?'

My ancestors tut so loudly in the dark, it makes me flinch.

I look at her.

'I became an actor because I wanted to be free.'

Long pause. The spirits of the past walk slowly, feet dragging them to their resting places once more. I suddenly remember the name of Simba's mom in *The Lion King*. Sarabi. It means 'mirage' in Swahili.

Of course. Of course.

We look at each other in silence.

EXT. LONDON. DAWN.

The crisp dawn air hits ACTRESS*'s lungs,*
as she walks aimlessly along a canal.
It's not clear whether she's been up all
night, where she's coming from or where
she's headed. Her hair blows limply in
the breeze as she pulls her usual mac
around her.

She stops, stares into the water for a
long time. Her reflection, blurry, moves
on the water's surface. The birds sing.

MALE JOGGER *jogs past. He double-takes*
as he passes ACTRESS*. He jogs backwards.*
Stands next to ACTRESS*.*

                    MALE JOGGER
               (*in a hushed voice*)
          Business?

ACTRESS *turns slowly.*

                    MALE JOGGER
            (*looking around, stretching,*
                    loud voice)
          Yeah, it is a nice morning. (*hushed*
          voice) Business?

ACTRESS *stares at him.*

> MALE JOGGER
> (*looks around, loud voice*)
> Yeeeah, I always take this route.
> Beautiful, isn't it? (*hushed voice*)
> Business?

ACTRESS *is silent. She cocks her head to one side. The birds sing.*

> MALE JOGGER
> (*hushed voice*)
> Business? *Business?* (*loud voice*)
> Haha! Yeah, that's it, you've got to
> keep fit! (*hushed voice*) Business?

ACTRESS *deliberately tightens the belt on her mac.*

> MALE JOGGER
> (*hushed voice*)
> For fuck's sake, business?

ACTRESS *bends down slowly.*

> MALE JOGGER
> (*excited*)
> Yeah? Yeah?

ACTRESS *slowly removes her trainers.*

                    MALE JOGGER
                  (*loud voice*)
        Yeah! Exactly. Haha!(*hushed voice*)
        What are you doing?

ACTRESS *sits on the edge of the canal.*
Dangles her feet in the water.

                              CUT TO:

Character: Suzette, 30+.
Breakdown: An alluring European beauty
who brings grown men to their knees.
Project: Theatre/Broadway.
Notes from casting: French accent
required.

Auditions. Asking strangers for unconditional love. It's precarious. They are fear fests for me. Always have been. Too tall, too fat, too brown, too quirky, not talented, too talented, not loud enough, not silent enough, not photogenic, not chatty, not sexy, not special, too young, too old, too nervous, too sluggish, too uptight, too London, too posh, too funny, eyes too big, brain too big – you learn to pick up thoughts telepathically in the tiny rooms they cram you into.

Auditions are always in awkward spaces, with few exceptions. Churches, Masonic halls, windowless basements, disused loft space. Today I sit outside a small room in a prefab office block near a motorway. I reread the script. An intimate three-hander with a female lead. A French immigrant living in New York, a junior lawyer who starts a love affair with the underground jazz scene in the Big Apple. The syncopated rhythms inspire her to break her corporate chains and form a three-way relationship with two American men, both musicians. The men and the music unlock her subliminally and the plot thickens when painful memories of an abusive father start to surface. The music is her saviour and her tormentor. There's lots to discuss.

In the room, the writer/director is a brooding figure, no smile or handshake. He sits with his hands clasped on a plastic chair in front of a long table of men and women I don't recognise and who don't introduce themselves. The casting director, who I've known for years, isn't present today, the writer/director is doing it all himself. I try to make conversation about the weather and he tells me to get my script out in response. It's always a gamble as to how much preamble you get at the start of an audition – I've talked for half an hour about what I had for breakfast before reciting a line of script and I've had people silently direct my attention to signs that outline 'no touching or hugging', before starting in on the scenes. Today is another extreme. The director suggests we jump straight into one of the bleakest scenes of the whole script, a three-page monologue towards the end of the play about the abuse the character suffered for most of her childhood. It's a heavy place to start, especially with my dodgy French accent still warming up.

'Come on, time is money,' he says, with all the pace and urgency of a New Yorker.

I pull my chair to the middle of the room and flip through my earmarked pages.

I've barely finished my first line before the director starts shouting from across the room. I look up. He tells me not to look at him, to look at the scene.

'Get into that *place*, come on!'

I keep going.

'You're *not* crying!'

I'm not crying, he's right, I'm three sentences in.

'You're talking about some dark stuff here! What *Daddy* did to you! You should have tears streaming down your face!'

I'm not sure how many abused women this director has met. I've met a few. To suggest that tears are a signifier of how they feel about their childhoods being robbed from them is naive – to use a polite word.

'Come on, come on! Give it to me!'

Now I feel like I'm in a porn film.

'Give it to me, come on! *Really get into it!*'

I pause. He shouts louder. I keep going. *Why* do I keep going? I look at the people behind the table. I'm guessing it's their money that my time sat here not crying is wasting.

'Come on, come on!'

They watch in silence, not moving or blinking. If they're androids, they're not in the least bit convincing as humans. The shouting and my own voice reciting the lines create a wall of sound that is genuinely disturbing. If someone happened to be listening outside the door, they'd have good reason to call the police.

'Come on, come on, come on, *come on*!'

I see some saliva fly from his mouth.

The monologue culminates in some actually very badly written images of this woman's last days of abuse.

Graphic images that, when I say them out loud, do have an effect. How could they not? Instead of a measured confessional, this is a shouting match. The words on the page start to move. The room starts to move. The heat builds behind my eyes and I do cry.

'That's it, come on, come on, come on! You're there, you're there!'

He thinks he's rocking my world. I float above myself, watch him, wild, the reddest neck I've ever seen, and me, on the chair, script shaking and black spots of wet mascara on my shirt.

I stop. It's the end of the monologue. The end of lots of things.

'See what happened there? You *connected*.'

'Yup.'

What I want to say is that I'm crying because I'm *shredded* of connection. My senses are in a coffee grinder and he's mistaken it for good direction.

'Is that it?'

I don't wait for an answer. Like a baby learning to walk, I push myself off objects to get across the room. I push myself off the chair seat to stand. I use the back of the chair to pivot towards the door. I pick up my bag and coat from the floor and use them as weights to balance me so I don't fall down. I let gravity pull me forward until I'm face-to-face with the door. It's when I'm trying to negotiate how to lift one of my arms to get at the door handle that I hear the music. It starts slowly. My nose is nearly touching the door frame. I look down at my hands that are clutching my things and think, This is it. I might never see these things again. I'm thinking, It's happened. I've crossed over. I'm down the rabbit hole. I'm hearing music. Can I smell burnt toast? Has someone already called the paramedics? Is that what I'm hearing? Sirens made musical? I pushed myself too far, I should have stopped, but I carried on and now I'm caving in. The music continues to play.

'Come on, come on, get into it ...'

A whisper from across the room.

'Just let it take you.'

Does he mean the ambulance?

'Dance for me.'

My head moves independently from my body; it turns slowly like a possessed owl towards the sound. Eyes roll back from their sockets hoping to see a stretcher and a team of professionals ready with gas and air. Why is there a *boom box* on the table? Have I been transported back to the eighties? The music plays on. The director is finger-snapping to the beat. He looks like an ogre from a fairy tale, luring me with sweet music to my final resting place under the enchanted bridge. Jazz floats on the air.

'Just let your body go, come on. Feel it.'

The androids are looking at me. They can't compute why I'm not moving. Everyone is looking at me. They all want me to – dance – for them? My legs bend. No, don't do that! One leg steps forward independently of me. What the hell? I look down – my bag and coat are back on the floor. My hands are betraying me too, they can't be serious. I can feel them moving by my sides, spiralling up my body, making shapes independently in the air around me. The androids now have their faces set to 'dead-eyed smile'. My hips are moving?

'That's it, good. You're in 1920s Brooklyn, you're in a smoky bar and all eyes are on you. You *know* they're on you, girl.'

So I've died and am on the slow descent to hell. That's what's happening here. I'm in the back of the ambulance, nearly dead. My arms continue to move. I think I might even spin. I say, *I*. I'm not sure who's captain of this ship any more. Then the music changes, or is that my life-support machine flatlining?

'It's now the thirties, you're raging, you're in your element!'

Some drums come in loud, some big-band swing, the tribal drums and screeching trumpet should make me fall to my knees in my fragile condition, but the puppet master has me dangling in time to the beat now.

'Atta girl!'

I snap my fingers, like him. I think my legs are can-canning? Now my hands and knees have decided to charleston. I'm dead, so what do I care?

The music changes again. It's an era-spanning megamix. I remember now. On the front of the script there was a quote, from a famous musician I think – something about music being the only thing that connects us to our past. Oh my God. He's getting me to *dance through time*.

'It's now the forties, forget the thirties. There's a war on!'

A woman's voice starts to croon out of the speakers, backing singers in perfect harmony echo her every phrase. Hands clap, fingers click on the record, the sound of my spirit snapping. 'A little bird told me we'd be happy/I believed it was true,' croons the woman and her band. The piano is jumpy and excitable. I can feel my shoulders moving up and down, my body swaying sexlessly like a white forties music-hall singer. I'm smiling, my elbows moving in and away from my body as my fingers fan out in front of me, making two jazz hands. I move in a slow circle, a dancing ghost. I catch a glimpse of the androids, the whites of their expressionless eyes. The music changes era once more.

'Here we are.'

The fifties arrive, and with them comes one of the most heart-breaking jazz divas of the time. A Billie elegy. The exquisite pain rises up and out of the crude speakers and there's no instinct to dance. My arms reach up and around myself, slowly. I hug myself. My eyes close, my head lolls and falls to one side, my hair covers one of my eyes, I let my head roll back occasionally, like a newborn. I let my neck *ache*. I slow-dance with myself and with my sister on the record, let the piano enter me, send me to heaven. I breathe it out of my lungs. I let the melancholy of that woman's voice bewitch them for me.

'Yes, feel it.'

He has no clue. This isn't *for you* and this music isn't to be *felt*, it's to be obliterated by. When the era changes again, I feel stronger. The defibrillator must be on my chest in the back of this ambulance because my body feels able. The sixties strike up. Some boys with long hair and guitars, African-American girls on the backing track giving them soul. I jump up and down like a bunny, foot to foot, Lindy hop, hands make generalised psychedelic shapes.

'Yeah! Yeah!'

I look at him in the eyes, through his expensive tinted glasses. My cheeks wobbling up and down. You want me to dance? I'll dance. I'll dance until this roof falls in on your head. I want this terrible idea to kill you.

The seventies now – how the hell has he made this mix? The boom box crackles out some generic Motown. I make my fingers into peace signs and pass them over my eyes. Backwards, forwards, backwards, forwards, stare out through them at the androids, wishing their heads would explode. The eighties, wow, it's all here – it's time for some easy-listening R&B. I let my shoulders get ridiculous. Let one dive up towards my ear and back down, let the other one do the same. Let my breasts jiggle violently under my shirt, shake me, pull me, rock me. I let my fake smile become terrifying and roll my head from side to side, imagine an extended eighties high ponytail whipping through the air.

'Feel it! Feel it!'

I'd like the next song to inspire projectile vomit so I can watch it dribble down those jazzy specs. The nineties and I'm at my most manic. A Jennifer Lopez-style synthesised Latin pop number fills the room. I comedy salsa. Make my mouth into a pursed 'O' shape as I *roll* one hip forward, then the other, then again. Let the synthetic sex of it stink up the room. I twist, dip and hip and twist and fake body roll, shake my booty – rhumba! I'm vibrating like a fake Latina pop star. Hair swish, hand through hair, dip and twist, dip and twist, leg lock, arms up, windmill arms, smile, head bang, pump pump pump my pelvis. Why isn't the plaster from the roof beginning to drop? I've come back to life with superhuman strength! I press my tongue against my teeth and scream. The music stops. My panting is audible. My dehydrated gulps. What about the noughties? Some Blazin' Squad? Come on, let's do this properly!

'Thank you.'

The androids stare back, unmoved.

'No more? I can keep going.'

'Yeah. That's the end of the tape. Thank you.'

He's dismissing me. Looking at me like I've lost control. Like he's *embarrassed* for me. He's asking me to leave the way a barman would ask a drunk woman to. One who's spent the night giving her free tequila shots and then is horrified when she tries to dance on a table. I pick up my bag, my coat. The room is eerily silent. I walk down the long spiral staircase and straight into an old-fashioned sandwich shop across the road. I don't put my coat on, I just walk. I order a cheese sandwich and a coffee and sit in one of the booths. Pop music plays out of a small stereo behind the counter. I lay my face on the cold plastic.

INT. TRAVEL AGENT'S OFFICE,
HIGH STREET. DAY.

ACTRESS *browses the holiday brochures,*
drops a couple on the floor.

> SATURDAY GIRL
Can I help you?

> ACTRESS
Sorry, I was just a bit confused for
a minute there.

> SATURDAY GIRL
Can I help?

> ACTRESS
Didn't this used to be a funeral
director's? For people who'd died.
Abroad. It was a special service to
bring bodies home from the Caribbean
and Latin America?

> SATURDAY GIRL
Oh, yes!

                    ACTRESS
Now it's the reverse. It's for people
to go away and 'come alive', as your
sign says.

                 SATURDAY GIRL
Well, exactly, yes! Why don't you sit
down? What kind of trip did you have
in mind?

                    ACTRESS
I'm not sure, really. I wanted to
know what my options were. I mean,
maybe the Caribbean or Latin America?

                 SATURDAY GIRL
Sit down, sit down.

ACTRESS *sits.*

                 SATURDAY GIRL
So what are your priorities?

                    ACTRESS
Spiritual awakening?

SATURDAY GIRL *looks at her.*

Pause.

SATURDAY GIRL
I can certainly search that for you.

ACTRESS
Warm, warm is also good. I just need
some rest.

SATURDAY GIRL
R&R, got you, lovely.

ACTRESS
What's the other R — again?

SATURDAY GIRL
Relaxation.

ACTRESS
That's it. That's what I want.

SATURDAY GIRL
Oookay, what's your budget?

ACTRESS
Good, I'm glad you asked. It's not a
lot. It's not much.

SATURDAY GIRL

Oookay. For a low budget at this time
of year, are you happy to stay in
England?

ACTRESS

I was thinking something more remote.
Jungle, the desert?

SATURDAY GIRL

Caravans can be quite spiritual?

CUT TO:

Character: Patty, 30+.
Breakdown: The village mute leads an army to battle. Her frailty becomes her strength. Lead.
Project: Fantasy/feature/first in the franchise.
Notes from casting: Although there are no lines for this character, this is a great role for any woman. Wardrobe and hair will be very striking.

I'm alive and *my voice* is dead.

I went to sleep and found it dead on arrival the next morning.

It, like me, is tired. I'm scared, really scared, but can't show it. I have to be strong for my voice, set an example. I whisper to it, like a friend. I tell it that I'm sorry I've been working it so hard. I tell it that I appreciate how much it's been carrying me through a West End run. I tell it that it was very kind of it, despite me not treating it to proper drugs when it first got sick, to have kept going. I coo at it, drench it in honey. It doesn't talk back. It sounds loud in my head, but when I open my mouth it crackles out, like the end of a record. Occasionally there will be a buzzing sound, but I can't control when. It's overthrown me. The show has gone on, until it can't.

A professional takes a photograph of my vocal cords. I see my nemesis close up on a screen. Two angry, red swellings where smooth pink vocal folds used to be. The two folds have been punching each other instead of sliding up against one another like a kiss. The wounds have filled with pus and now I can't talk. Why are they angry at each other? Angry at me? We started performing when we were so young, maybe they've retired inside me, departed to a condo in Florida and left these dry lumps in their place.

'Six days in silence starting now. No gesturing. Even miming can do damage as your vocal cords will still try to form the word.'

I can't even protest! I swallow hard and take my prescription for special fluids to the pharmacy. They smile knowingly when I slide the scrunched paper wordlessly over the counter.

People pay for this kind of thing. Silent retreats. They go to beaches in Goa to connect with their inner voice, letting emotions surface and the sea cleanse them. I'm going to do this on a sofa in Hackney. Taking time off the show is bad enough. I don't have children, I can't imagine what it's like to have a child, my friends who are mothers would hit me if I said it out loud, but it feels like I've left my baby somewhere. I remember one time when my mum forgot that my baby brother was in a baby carrier on the roof of the car. When I yelled that he was still up there before we went to the supermarket, I can still remember so vividly the look she gave me. A deeply sunken look.

A look that said, 'I am bad person. Bad to the core.' That look is how I feel right now.

Thankfully, people seem to respond especially well to mutes. It's the kindest I've ever seen my fellow Londoners. People mime and whisper in solidarity with me, it moves me to tears often. There's this immediate connection when your only form of communication is non-verbal. It's a sensory overload. Every time I leave the house, my whole body, my whole face has to scream what it is I desire. Even if it's just a flat white. It's overwhelming. It's like being a baby again. My eyes are becoming more and more intense by the day. I look in the mirror and they look desperate, a little crazed even, like a silent movie star. They're having to be overexpressive for too long and they're sticking that way. What I could really do with is some subtitles.

At first, if I have to write anything down for people, I use pen and paper. It turns out that's a little too Charles Dickens for the average stranger. They tend to shake their heads and walk away, assuming you're begging. I try not to take it personally and start to write all my notes on my phone. When you approach people with technology, their reception is always warm. They expect you to show them a map, or some digital directions to something. Then they read my little note: *Hello, I've lost my voice – can you help me?* – and there's nothing they won't do. They smile and touch me, taxi drivers run round and open doors. The kindness of strangers becomes a drug.

I still don't want my voice to get used to it though, to get too comfortable in its silent cage. I want to scratch my skin off it's so quiet sometimes. On the fifth day I can feel the impulse to speak fading altogether, which has me weeping silently into a pillow. At the start I would get these little stabbing pains just below my stomach. It was the impulse to make words. My head would jerk forwards, a reflex that my brain had to shut down. Sometimes my leg would kick out randomly, trapped words trying to get out. Now the impulse has gone. I don't twitch to speak, I become human mashed potato and watch atrocities on the news, reality-TV sing-offs, all day without comment. My dreams, which were at the start of the silence lucid and sometimes terrifying, suddenly become as muted as I am. My brain is sludge. My breathing is shallow. My breath constantly smells. Not least because I'm experimenting with the natural anti-inflammatory effects of white onion and turmeric. I'm attempting to drink six litres of water a day so spend a lot of time in my toilet. I don't even read any more, just sit and listen enviously to the chirping city birds. I'm even jealous at the zingy sound of my own jet of piss. It rings in my ears.

On the morning of the seventh day, I head back to the specialist. I take a cab. Being outside has become a little too loud for me. As soon as I sit down, he asks me to speak. I stiffen.

'Say something. Anything. Full voice.'

I wanted to speak so much! But now I've got the chance I don't know what to say. What's the right way to break the spell? I'm scared of my own voice. I don't know it any more. What if it's changed? What if the sound that comes out is that of a tiny baby? Or a terrifying ogre? My heart is racing. The words are in my throat, they're burning, my chest vibrates with suppressed noise. My knees twitch, knock against each other. I close my eyes.

'Whatever you do, don't whisper.'

That sounds like something from a scary folk tale. The girl who was silent and is asked to speak for the first time, whispers and her voice is trapped forever. She's doomed to sound like a dormouse for the rest of her life.

'It's a muscle that's been rested and needs to get straight back on the field.'

I open my eyes and look at the specialist. I ask my voice what it wants to say. Ask it to come back to life as it sees fit, not to worry about me.

'Hello? This is my voice.'

The words take me by surprise. So does the sound. I sound like someone I used to know.

'Very good!'

I laugh tears.

Suddenly unemotional, he shuts my file. He lubes up a long metal tube with a camera at the end and manoeuvres it down my throat.

'Say aaaah, oooooh, eeeeh.'

It sounds so much better. He snaps another photo. I hope my vocal cords have sent their young and attractive understudies. I realise with this cold tube in my mouth, how desperately I want to get back to work. How much I want to talk on the phone again.

The photograph up on the screen isn't perfect, but it's good enough. The witchy pustules have become pinker, smaller, cuter. My throat no longer looks like the Gates of Hell, but it's not out of Purgatory yet. I need speech therapy. I literally have to learn to speak again. Learn to breathe again. I still need to stay silent as much as possible. Ideally, until the show every night. The nightmare doesn't end but takes on a strange new form.

The speech therapist has a contraption that can tell you every quality and every tone you have in your voice. She asks me to speak into a microphone to measure – among other things – the 'shimmer' in my voice. I like that. I like to think of my voice retaining some shimmer in its hospital bed. I imagine glitter blowing softly onto the microphone head.

'Just say what you had for breakfast.'

'I haven't eaten yet.'

The silence and an appetite don't seem to go hand in hand.

Turns out my shimmer, among other things, is way down there. Range-wise.

'OK, so what these lines tell us, these numbers –' she points to a digital graph of my voice – 'is that your voice has become a good few decibels lower than the average male.'

I knew it was still husky, but not that husky.

'There's a lot of work to do.'

I want to scream.

'The first thing you really need to start with, when thinking about breath, is not thinking about it at all.'

She says there comes a time when our voices are vulnerable. When our self-expression becomes vulnerable for whatever reason, and our breath starts to over-compensate, overwork.

'If we have perhaps come to the conclusion that we are a person who is misunderstood, we can start to push our breath. We push the points we are trying to make, so that they might not be misinterpreted. If you have come to the conclusion that your voice isn't heard, you will have a tendency to underuse your breath. Your voice will whisper your thoughts so that they are just audible, but still very much under the radar. Keeping you safe, from shame.'

She tells me that my voice is my emotional self and I should communicate with it as such.

'I have been speaking to my voice. I felt mad for doing it, but that was my instinct.'

She turns the corners of her mouth down, moves her finger slowly side to side in the air.

278

'No, no, no, no, this is not insane. Who is telling us that this is insane?'

I shrug.

'We have to talk to our voices. We have to ask it to do what we want it to do. We have to make a promise to use it wisely. We have to acknowledge it and forget it at the same time.'

I walk out of the room, enlightened, to the theatre. I ask if my voice wants to hold my hand on the way.

Onstage, I suffer but I soldier. Offstage, I become obsessed with my voice and its secret emotional life. I want to find out more. I become like a mum stalking her child on Facebook. I want to know *who* it is when it's not with me. I want to know if I've raised it right. I've been the sole person looking after this voice all these years and it's suddenly turned against me. Why? Is it hanging out with the wrong crowd, taking drugs? As well as the stalking, I seek every alternative remedy I can find – on behalf of my voice. There's a wondrous woman who I saw for acupuncture for years. She's managed to rekindle the spark between lots of different parts of my body so far. She reintroduced me to my brain at one point, when it looked like anxiety was going to drive a wedge between us.

When I go back, she wants to know what took me so long.

'Acupuncture not just for emergency!' She wags her finger. 'It's for your life!'

She asks about my life, about the work I'm doing, my personal life, my family life. One of her most pressing questions is whether I'm doing enough singing and dancing.

'It lifts the chest, calms the spirit.'

'It's my chest that brings me here. My voice really.'

'Your lungs,' she corrects me. 'Chinese medicine is about the source, not the symptom.'

I tell her about the two angry polyps that have taken up residency in my vocal folds. I expect a prescription for some specialist teas and herbs. Instead she thinks long and hard, observing me, offers me a diagnosis.

'The truth has got stuck in your throat.'

'There's truth stuck *in* my throat?'

'Something you're afraid to say. It has become stuck – like you.'

She laughs. She has a habit of doing that. She often takes the power of her own words for granted.

I see the truth inside my throat like crumpled paper stuffed down into a wastebasket.

'Speak your truth. Get better.'

I don't think I can take any more emotion. I also notice that when I become emotional now, it goes straight to my throat. It dries up and stings like a not-long-dead wasp. What have I been holding back?

I scroll through the notes on my phone, my discordant messages to strangers and loved ones alike. The chaos of them is thrilling, telling. It's like looking at my-self through a broken kaleidoscope.

Pick up some white wine
Have you got a crush?
Who are hipsters?
Snacks?
Have to work out where my next job is coming from
Shall I do yoga?
Cappuccino
Thanks for helping
I'm not a quitter but am powerless
I always planned to wear this T-shirt
It's all gone to shit
Europe is much less prejudiced about ageing electro
    rockers
Have I lost weight in 9 weeks?
Black Prime Minister!!!!
I've got no money left
More Tracy Chapman
It's all bullshit as we know
See good films?
I'm broken
Nice to see you
Proud doesn't cover it
This woman is not memorable
Coca-Cola?
High bikini please
Love you too will really miss you

I'm in fear constantly

Mum wanted you to bring a white wine

We can do the glamorous photo later

AMERICA deadline

Thai green curry please

Cringing in my bum

Deeply

Moved audition, too much

Funny how your context can change your personality

Don't make me laugh

You can't do these things as a woman of colour

Moved audition – too much

Don't tell anyone

Sobriety, it's worked a treat

Don't pat me on the arm

Broken

Porridge

You look well otherwise

I washed her duvet cover

Shall I go to the audition?

What can I do about boobs coming out?

Remember when you said you wanted to slap me on
    the head?

I can't even mouth words

Nudity and incest!

Do I need to see a doctor?

There's a point where a Snickers isn't enough

The emotional shopping list of a tragic silent movie star. Where to begin? I don't see much truth in here other than perhaps cutting back on white wine?

I talk to my voice again, hoping it'll hear me.

'What do *you* want me to say?'

INT. ACTRESS'S BEDROOM. EARLY AFTERNOON.

ACTRESS, *wearing a mac and a pair of novelty heart-shaped sunglasses, sits on the edge of the bed. Her coat is still wet from the rain. She tears the plastic from an international calling card and scratches the silver strip. She punches the codes into her phone. Goes through the relevant steps. She dials. After a few moments* GRANDMOTHER *picks up. We hear her as a voice-over.*

GRANDMOTHER

Hello?

ACTRESS

Hello, Jajja! ('*Grandmother*' *in Luganda.*)

GRANDMOTHER

My dear, my dear, my dear — how are you?

ACTRESS

I just wanted to hear your voice. You recognised *my* voice?

GRANDMOTHER
Of course, my dear!

ACTRESS
Ha! I don't recognise it myself at
the moment.

GRANDMOTHER
I love to hear your voice.

ACTRESS
And I love to hear *yours*.

GRANDMOTHER
How are you, my dear?

ACTRESS
I'm fine. I'm fine. How are you?

GRANDMOTHER
I'm fine too. My legs hurt from time
to time.

ACTRESS
Really? I'm sorry to hear that.

GRANDMOTHER
My age. You sound tired, dear.

                    ACTRESS
       Oh?

ACTRESS *takes the phone away from her*
mouth. She coughs, takes her voice up a
pitch.

                    ACTRESS
       I'm fine! What's happening there?

                    GRANDMOTHER
       We're all well, thank God.

                    ACTRESS
       It must be the morning there? You
       must be getting ready!

                    GRANDMOTHER
       What?

                    ACTRESS
       Do you have make-up on? Your handbag?

                    GRANDMOTHER
                      (*off*)
       I can't hear her.

                    ACTRESS
       I'm here!

GRANDMOTHER

How are you, my dear? How is work?

ACTRESS

Work is great. I just wanted to see
how you are. How everyone there is.

GRANDMOTHER

I'm going to church, my dear. Can you
hear me?

ACTRESS

I can hear you, Jajja!

GRANDMOTHER

(*off*)

I can't hear her. (*to* ACTRESS) It's a
bad line, my dear. I love you very much.

ACTRESS

I love you too.

GRANDMOTHER

May you always be blessed.

ACTRESS

You too. Jajja? Can I ask something?

GRANDMOTHER

My dear?

ACTRESS

Do you ever feel eyes on you?

GRANDMOTHER

It's a bad line. (*Pause.*)
Everyone is so proud of you here.
Your career. Your aunties show me
the magazines. Do you remember when
you used to practise your reflections
in the mirror?

ACTRESS

Oh my God!

GRANDMOTHER

'I want to be everything!' You had
a strong voice for a child. And now
look.

ACTRESS

Thank you, Jajja. I've been thinking
about a visit, actually. I've been
working very hard and I think it's
time to take some time out, have a
rest.

                    GRANDMOTHER
Well, if you're sure you can spare
the time, dear. We'd love to see you,
dear!

                      ACTRESS
Ha! I can spare the time. I love you.

                    GRANDMOTHER
                 (*makes kiss sounds*)
Mwah, mwah, mwah, mwah, mwah, mwah.

                      ACTRESS
Mwah! Jajja?

                    GRANDMOTHER
Yes, my dear?

                      ACTRESS
Just double-checking, I just wanted
to ask.

                    GRANDMOTHER
Yes?

                      ACTRESS
Do you ever feel eyes on you?

                    GRANDMOTHER
          Hello?

                    ACTRESS
          Yes?

                    GRANDMOTHER
          Eyes?

                    ACTRESS
          Yes.

          Pause.

                    GRANDMOTHER
          Only God, my dear.

                                        CUT TO:

Character: Princess Pearl.
Breakdown: Princess of the sea, an ageless beauty.
Project: Fantasy/TV/first in the franchise.
Notes from casting: Please come with natural make-up and natural hair.

The sea has always called me.

Getting out of the house is hard, but getting to the beach seems to have been quite easy. The buses and the train and the speaking to the woman who owns the bed-and-breakfast – all painless.

I always lay my clothes out on the bed; it's a habit that won't die. I like making the clothes into the shape of the outfits, the shape of people. I lay both outfits out. A swimming costume tucked into jeans and a thick Christmas jumper with leggings. I tuck the Christmas jumper sleeve under the bum of the swimming costume and jeans. They look like young lovers. I put my toiletries out, a habit learned in the theatre. If you don't put your toiletries out on the first day in your dressing room, you never will. You have to make it a ritual, everything in its place. It has to feel holy, or you'll always struggle to get ready in good time. Cotton pads will mysteriously vanish when you need them, an eyeliner will go walkabout five minutes before curtain. You want to be in character at least half an hour before the show. I line up a squeezed-out facecloth and my toothbrush, a lip balm and some hair oil, my perfume. It surprises me how little I've packed. I refine their positions until they're in order of importance.

The light in the room has a distinct mood. There's an old-fashioned reading table and chair by the window. They're lit exactly like a play. The square of the window is exactly reflected on the low wall behind it. I sit in the chair. You know when you're in the right spot because the light illuminates everything inside your face. To be well lit is to feel immortal. I crook my elbow, and place my hand delicately under my chin. I stare out of the window with gentle eyes at the coastline. I let a hint of a smile cross my lips, coyly lower my eyes. I stroke the side of my face as though I'm alone, but being watched. I sigh the sigh of a mid-nineteenth-century muse, try and find my light again. When there's a sharp knock at the door, I run back to the bathroom and pick up my toothbrush.

'What time will you be wanting breakfast?'

My heart races.

'Any time is fine!'

There's a pause.

'All right, I'll put the hot food on at eight, help yourself to muesli and things like that.'

She creaks away. I put my toothbrush back in its sacred place and fill the novelty mother-of-pearl soap dish with my necklace and two rings. I need to swim. The anonymity of the sea.

*

I've walked the length of the road in bare feet. Soaking them at the water's edge feels – powerful. Pushing the shells of mussels and silky skimming stones down into the heavy sand, as I gently rock. I've gone for the swimsuit-and-jeans costume. I do my best to embody the 'Young Lover'. I throw my hands in the air and let the wind shake my hair back. I hop foot to foot, excited – as only a young lover at the seaside can be. I let the water soak the bottom of my turn-ups, and when they're too wet, I unzip my jeans and throw them on the sand with more abandon than has ever been usual for me. The tide is going out and I go with it. Wade in to my knees until they're so cold they're burning. The fear comes in waves, but I know I can't leave without going under. There's a steep drop and suddenly my thighs are under, my waist. Stagnant blood tingles as it's woken from a deep sleep. My breath is cut off as water smashes into my lower ribs. My back starts to spasm, totally alive. I visualise my head going under, the deep intake of breath – when there's a voice.

''Scuse me?'

I turn and half expect to find a talking seagull.

'Didn't you used to be someone?'

My feet are on fire with cold.

'Films and things? Can we get a selfie? For my daughter?'

She pulls the young girl out from behind her. The girl sucks her fist, looks at the ground.

'I was just about to go in.'

'It'll only take a sec.'

I look down at my thighs, they change shape under the surface.

'It would mean the world.'

Seagulls stare at me, hollow-eyed. I want to be alone.

'OK.'

I feel like Nessie, finally caught, wading through shame to dry land. I pick up my jeans, dry my legs. Hold them as a crumpled shield in front of my stomach as the woman preps her phone. The goosebumps on my arms are as hard as limpets on rock.

'Thank you so much.'

The three of us appear in the screen. The woman smiles brightly, the little one remains indifferent and I look – not like me. I haven't seen a picture of myself for a while. The eyes of the woman staring back at me are as troubling as the eyes of the seagulls. There, but not there. Piercing and fixed. My face is paler than it should be.

'Thank you so much, we love you. Thank you. Can I buy you a cup of tea?'

'I should get back in the water, it's colder out here. Weirdly.'

I smile enough to put an end to the conversation.

'Bye.'

'What's an actress?'

The little girl looks me dead in my dead eyes.

'Sorry, she asks things like that.'

I stare down into her eyes. My brain races. I can't answer.

'Puts people on the spot.'

'It's good to be curious.'

'Do they eat ice cream?'

The honesty cuts through me faster than the wind hitting my back.

'Do you want to come for a cup of tea? You shouldn't swim when the tide's going out anyway.'

I put my young lover jeans back on, without taking my eyes off the child.

The lady talks and talks, mostly about all the dreams she had before, before the kid. She litters the beach with her regrets. Her daughter makes a meal of collecting stones, but I can tell she hears everything.

'Do you have kids?'

The little girl looks at me through a hole in a chalky stone.

'We don't ask questions like that.'

I pick up a similar stone wedged in the sand and hand it to her.

'No, I don't.'

She turns the stone over in her hands.

'Do you want to have them?'

A sandfly scuttles over my foot. I don't jump.

'Yes, I do.'

We stop at every landmark along the promenade. The girl's mum wants more photos, but just of me and the kid now.

'I wanna go home,' she whines.

'That's very ungrateful, Bianca, we don't get opportunities like this every day, it isn't every day you get to meet someone famous. You'll look back on these photos.'

The little one lets out a dramatic sigh, her lips rolling like a miniature pony.

'She's just a grown-up lady in a swimming costume!'

The mum looks like she is about to disintegrate with shame.

'I'm so sorry, can you watch her for a sec?'

Before I can answer, the mum walks away fumbling in her bag. She stands a way off trying to hide her cigarette and lighter. The girl and I watch as she waves smoke erratically into the wind.

'She thinks she's invisible.'

We share a smile.

'Where's your shoes?'

She taps my toes with her little boots.

'I didn't feel like wearing them.'

'Is that what actresses do?'

'Sometimes. Usually it's about putting clothes *on*.'

'Do you believe in Santa?'

'Yes.'

'Good. Some people say he's pretend.'

'That's some people.'

'Stupid people.'

She waits for a telling-off, tests me.

'An actress is like Santa. Sometimes they're pretend, sometimes they're real. I'm like that. Your mum.'

She's restless, kicking a lamp post.

'I don't like that. Have you got money for an ice cream?'

'No, I haven't.'

'Any *pretend* money?'

We laugh.

'Here you go.'

I take the pretend money out of my pocket. Put it in her hand.

'This will get us loads of ice cream!'

She passes me a huge bowl.

'Ten different flavours, all your favourites!'

I take them, being so careful to mime them exactly.

'All my favourites! How did you know?'

'What *is* your favourite?'

'I'm not sure. I don't know.'

She picks up her own bowl and mimes ice-cream mountains going into her mouth. Squeals with delight, bounces her knees.

'You look happy.'

She studies my face, makes sure I'm telling the truth. I mime licking ice cream off my lips. I make cartoon slurping sounds.

'You look happy too.'

I smile.

'What do you want to be when you grow up?'

She looks up at me, moves her eyes before her head. Makes it dramatic.

'Everyone asks that!'

She throws the pretend bowl on the ground. I've burst the fragile bubble that was ours and only ours.

'Sorry.'

'That's what everyone always asks.'

'I'm so sorry. Here, have one of my flavours.'

She shakes her head.

'I want to be everything.'

Her mum takes her hand and apologises for any nuisance she might have caused. She's a spirited child and it runs her ragged.

The little girl takes my imaginary bowl, expertly, and lays it on the ground.

The long walk back is bracing. It's been nice to be free from shoes, but my feet have small cuts on them. I stare at the sea and it doesn't stare back. The tide looks like it's coming in, so I run across the road. This time, there's no one to see me in the near-dark. I am as excited as a child. The soles of my feet sting with joy. They want to feel it all. Want to feel the slap of it and the freezing cold and the seaweed. I get past the freezing-hot stage quicker this time, my ankles aren't afraid, neither are my calves or my thighs. I jump into the water chest first, like I'm hugging it. It comes up to meet me. Doesn't care who I am. It rocks me. My shoulders spasm as the cold settles in. I can't get my breath, but in the good way. Gasping for air makes me feel free. There's no one watching. The black water used to scare me. I stare into it with the eyes of fish, try and penetrate it, see all the way. Pieces of seaweed fly past my cheeks, I can't believe I'm not screaming! I surface and take another lungful, smash my head in again, determined to see through this dark water. I stretch my eyes, open them as far as they will go. Nothing. Nothing. I dunk my head in and out, holding my breath and staring at the deepest point. Until the not-seeing becomes the seeing. I can't see anything, nothing shows itself to me and that becomes the beauty. There's ages and ages and leagues and leagues of nothing. My lungs are bursting now. Ribs are trying to escape skin. I yank my head out and try and take the sea with me, catch it all in my hair. A spray of saltwater traces the sky. I shake my head, let it whip it across my back, my shoulders, across my face, it sounds like seaweed slapping me awake. I kick my legs up and over the water, run back to the shore like a kid. I'm alone. In the night on the beach, I'm alone. No one else. I'm not beside myself, or behind myself, or ahead of myself.

INT. WOMAN PRODUCER'S HOUSE, SOUTH OF
THE RIVER. DAY.

ACTRESS *stands at the door of a large
Victorian terrace. She smooths her hair.
A woman answers the door. This is* WOMAN
PRODUCER.

> WOMAN PRODUCER
> I'm so glad you could make it.
> Come inside, please.

> ACTRESS
> Sure.

WOMAN PRODUCER *leads* ACTRESS *upstairs.*

> WOMAN PRODUCER
> Have you travelled far?

> ACTRESS
> Quite far. Yes, quite far.

> WOMAN PRODUCER
> I promise I won't take up much of
> your time.

WOMAN PRODUCER *opens the door to a
light-filled loft room at the top of the*

house. *Abstract female bodies on huge canvases are propped up against the walls, art-house film posters by all the female greats take up whatever space is left.*

They sit on two low chairs around a large coffee table. A script sits in the centre of it. We can see the title: Herself.

A camera stands on a tripod in the corner. ACTRESS *takes it all in, sits down, her breathing becomes shallow, trust ebbing away.*

> ACTRESS
> I thought — I'm sorry, I thought
> this was just — I'm not — really —
> prepared for —

WOMAN PRODUCER *turns, looks at the tripod.*

> WOMAN PRODUCER
> No. Don't worry, this isn't about —
> that at all. I'm not auditioning you.

> ACTRESS
> Oh?

                    WOMAN PRODUCER
As I said in my email, I like what
you do, always have. I wanted to
meet you, hear you read some of the
script. Just you and me. The part is
yours. If you want it. I'm sorry,
I thought I'd made that — clear.
My error. I don't have an assistant
or anything like that yet. I'm a
company of one.

                    ACTRESS
There's no one else coming?

                    WOMAN PRODUCER
No.

                    ACTRESS
Oh.

                    WOMAN PRODUCER
Is that OK?

                    ACTRESS
That's OK.

                    WOMAN PRODUCER
Are you comfortable with that?

                    ACTRESS
Yes.

                  WOMAN PRODUCER
                    (*laughs*)
You don't look sure.

                    ACTRESS
I am. That — it's — that never
happens.

                  WOMAN PRODUCER
I like people to feel comfortable.

                    ACTRESS
Which is ironically making me very
nervous.

WOMAN PRODUCER *laughs again*.

                  WOMAN PRODUCER
There's no need to be nervous.
Did you have any thoughts on the
script? Any feedback would be most
welcome.

                    ACTRESS
Can I be honest?

                    WOMAN PRODUCER
Oh dear.

                         ACTRESS
No, ha. No ... I didn't read it.
I love what you do very much too.
I always have. I wanted to meet you
too and tell you that ... I don't
do — this — any more. I don't ...

                    WOMAN PRODUCER
Take meetings?

                         ACTRESS
Act. Now.

                    WOMAN PRODUCER
Oh.

                         ACTRESS
Sorry.

                    WOMAN PRODUCER
Don't be sorry.

Tears prick ACTRESS*'s eyes.*

                         ACTRESS
Sorry.

                    WOMAN PRODUCER
          Don't be sorry.

                       ACTRESS
          I hadn't said it out loud yet.

WOMAN PRODUCER *gets up and grabs a
tissue from her immaculate desk that
seems to have everything you could ever
need in a creative crisis.*

ACTRESS *wipes her eyes, surprised at
herself. They sit in empathetic silence.*

                       ACTRESS
          I did notice, in the email, that
          there was no character breakdown.

                    WOMAN PRODUCER
          No. I don't write those.

ACTRESS *spontaneously laughs.*

                       ACTRESS
          Wow.

                    WOMAN PRODUCER
          I started out as an actress. I was
          OK, I worked enough, but I fell out

of love with it. And your heart has
to be in it, somewhere.

WOMAN PRODUCER *smiles, gets up and*
opens a drawer in the immaculate desk.
Produces a piece of paper, clearly
folded and unfolded, crumpled and un-
crumpled a hundred times. She hands the
piece of paper to ACTRESS. ACTRESS *opens*
it slowly.

It reads:

Character Breakdown

I need a woman who is happy with full
nudity and simulated sex who will be
FEATURED.

The character you would be playing is
murdered (off-screen). Before that, she
will be seen topless in one scene where
she is acting in a porn film — so you
must be comfortable simulating sex for
this scene. You will need to be prepared
to expose all on set, in order to make
it work. You would need to be completely
happy to simulate sex, kiss, simulate
groping/simulate being groped. She will

then be seen naked on a mortuary slab in another scene. FULL NUDITY is required for this.

>   WOMAN PRODUCER
>   They don't make 'em like that any
>   more.

She smiles.

>   WOMAN PRODUCER
>   When I decided to set up on my own,
>   I thought about framing it. For my
>   desk, there.

ACTRESS *folds the paper along the lines it's been folded and unfolded along before and slowly begins to tear the paper into very small strips. She throws them above her head —*

>   ACTRESS
>   Woo!

They float around her like dying fireworks.

>   ACTRESS
>   It's raining men!

WOMAN PRODUCER *laughs, a real laugh.*

                    ACTRESS
Ha! I'm so sorry.

                    WOMAN PRODUCER
Don't apologise.

                    ACTRESS
Do you have a bin?

                    WOMAN PRODUCER
Leave it there.

                    ACTRESS
Look — your lovely sofa —

                    WOMAN PRODUCER
                    (*still laughing*)
Stop.

                    ACTRESS
This is why —

                    WOMAN PRODUCER
Why —?

                    ACTRESS
    Why I don't, shouldn't do — it — any
    more. This is antisocial behaviour!
    I'm a danger to myself and to others!

WOMAN PRODUCER *is still laughing.*
ACTRESS *laughs with her.*

A *natural silence.*

                    ACTRESS
        Is this it?

ACTRESS *picks up* WOMAN PRODUCER*'s*
script.

                WOMAN PRODUCER
        In your own time.

ACTRESS *turns to the first page and*
begins to read.

Acknowledgements

Thank you to Eugenie Furniss and Emily Hayward-Whitlock for creating and supporting this special opportunity. To Becky Hardie for having the patience of a saint, you kept pushing, and I am very grateful. To the Chatto family for the incredible welcome. To all my acting representatives past and present – thank you for all your hard work and above all kindness. To Sandy Rees. To all the teachers who've believed in me, when I didn't believe in myself, particularly Chris Baron. To Anna Scher, my first ever drama teacher, who taught us that we must, where possible, put the *act* into *activism*.

Mum and Dad, thanks for the unshakeable belief and the deep-seated love of stories: I love you so much. Sam and Amy, everything I do is still motivated by trying to impress you, I think. Thank you for your art and, of course, jokes: I love you. My extended family (especially my jajja), whether near or far, for all the positive vibrations. To those we have lost, you are dearly missed and never forgotten. My friends. Especially Claire.

The beloved who held me up through this, thank you, you know exactly who you are. I literally couldn't have done this without you.